Evolutionary Feminism

MARY WAS THERE

Women in Struggle Slavery to Post Modernism

Evolutionary Feminism

Mary Was There

Women in Struggle Slavery to post Modernism

By Tufail Dhana

Published by

Create Space Amazon USA

Dedication

Dedicate to

Women of the World working for development of equality Pace and Justice

Acknowledgements

It is a small book with big story. It is story of women and women struggle. It is the story of struggle for freedom. Yes, women lost freedom in the war of slavery, almost twelve thousand years ago. Slavery affected human society as a disease. Women was degraded and dishonored by males. Even then, she contributed in development.

I am pleased. I have completed my book on the history of women. It is history of women struggle against slavery. I am thankful to my friends. They helped me. My family supported me. I am grateful to my wife, Rubina. I am very much thankful to my son, Hassan Bilal Dhana and Muhammad Junaid Dhana. They supported me. I have to say very much thank you to my younger son Muhammad Yousaf Dhana. He is always interested in my books. He asks many questions about my work. I am thankful to all, who have worked on struggle of women.

I am grateful to Amnat Bhutta, Yaseen Bhutta and Thameena Bhutta. My family friends in New York the provided me literature about women struggle. I am thankful Mr. Riaz Zahoor Khan *(Fiction House Publishers)*. He edited my book with experience and interest.

Contents

Preface   7

Introduction   9

1. War of Slavery   13

2. Slave Mothers   17

3. Saint House   19

4. Prostitute   24

5. Veil   28

6. Song of Tragedy   35

7. Sarah   39

8. The Royal Slave   42

9. Crisis of Iron Technologies   46

10. Suicide of Cleopatra   51

11. Mary Was There   56

12. Mother of Freedom   60

13. Classical Narrative   68

14. Classical Woman   73

15. Classical Wife   77

16. Classical Love   82

17. East and West   85

18. Narrative of Modernism   89

19. Women and Industrialization   93

20. Women in Modern Society   96

21. Weeping Mothers   99

22. Narrative of Post Modernism   104

23. Women in Struggle   107

24. Social Authority of Women   112

Preface

It is a small book which covers large span of women struggle in history. I wanted to right on this subject. I have completed. I am thankful to God. A writer learns in writing. I have learned much. It presents social evolution. It presents role of women in social development. There are stories about women, about the struggle of women. Women developed agriculture to feed family. She was made slave. Women fought for freedom. Saint Mary succeeded to defeat slavery. Woman is in struggle. She is in struggle for development of peace.

The book, you are going to read, states story of four civilizations. It presents woman in four civilizations. It presents social status and struggle of women from slavery to post-modernism. It states role of women in evolution and development of society. Woman was there in struggle of freedom. Saint Mary was there with Narrative of freedom. She defeated slavery. Cleopatra was at war of freedom against strong army of Romans. Author has been teaching as a professor in Biology. He obtained masters degree in Biology from University of the Punjab and joined college as a lecturer in 1988. Author has essential study and interest in evolution. *"Mary was there"* presents a study of women in history of social evolution. It is a reasonable book for students of 8-18 years. It is also for anybody interested to know about women struggle in development of society. *"Mary was there"* may be taken as evolutionary feminism in category.

Doctor Hassan Bilal Dhana

Introduction

Women in struggle, *"Mary was there"* is a research work of the author. It is about the role of women in social development. The book is on feminism in category. It is evolutionary feminism in opinion of the author. It presents story of women in the history of social evolution. There are about 25 stories to state struggle and status of women in history. War of slavery is first story. It was beginning of the tragedy in view of author. War of slavery appeared in Neolithic period almost 12 thousand years ago. Development of agriculture and trade of grain was basic cause of the war. Farmers wanted unpaid labor. They started war to collect slaves. They had developed a new narrative of life. The society was divided into masters and slaves. Slavery had reached climax. Greeks developed empire of slavery. Romans developed empire and culture of slavery. Saint Mary fought war of freedom against Romans.

Mary was mother of freedom. It is an important story in respect of content and concept. Author presents Saint Mary as mother of freedom. She fought a great war in history. She fought against Roman Empire of slavery. Mary fought against the

Narrative and culture of slavery. Jesus, the Christ, gave sacrifice of life for freedom of slaves. Author presents, Saint Mary was there behind the movement of Christianity. It was movement against slavery in reality. Mary was there present at the mount where Jesus was crucified. Mary was successful to win the war of freedom. Jupiter was defeated. Empire of slavery was defeated without sword. Christianity was not imposed by war. It was adopted by Roman Empire. It was a real miracle, in opinion of the author. Mary developed Narrative of freedom on the basis of Monism. She succeeded to negate Mythology and Idol worship. She negated the Narrative of slavery. Mary developed Narrative of Monism and freedom.

Classical civilization developed as a synthesis of freedom and slavery. Classical civilization was based on the divine Narrative. It was based on Monism. It was classified into classes on professional basis. Class division was permanent. Profession of the child was determined before birth. Author educates about classics and classical civilization. He educates about classical literature, music, and economy, political and social structure. Author states social status of women in classical society. Classical society was male dominated. Woman was domesticated. She was made servant. Classical wife and other stories present woman status in classical civilization.

Classical Narrative was challenged by modernism. It was

struggle of freedom. It appeared in Europe with renaissance. Narrative was based on modern science and technology. Modern philosophy developed ideology of rationalism to replace divinity. Modern science and technology developed modern economy. Invention of engine played big role. It developed industry. Modernism developed Nationalism and National state. National state was a constitutional state. Citizens found constitutional rights in the modern state. Modernity accepted the right of love and marriage. Woman was denied freedom of love in classical civilization.

Women participated in struggle of modernism. They worked in schools, hospitals and industry. Women participated in development of modern economy and social Narrative.

First wave of feminism appeared after industrial revolution. It was after 1850's. First wave of feminism addressed rights of women denied by male behavior. Women were treated as a female in continuity of classical Narrative. She was supposed responsible for parenting and domestic work. Women were paid less than male. Woman was not given the right for vote. She was denied political rights. First wave is known as suffrage movement. Women struggled for political rights in Europe.

Second wave of feminism appeared in 1960's. It was due to change in economic system. Corporations had dominated trade and industry in mid of 20th century. It created joblessness. Small industry was losing ground in competition with corporations. It affected workers. Woman was more affected because of crisis on small industry. Women appeared with struggle for equal salary and social rights.

Now women are active with third wave of feminism. Author states world is in change. World is changing in economical, political and social respects, in opinion of the author. It is post-modern phenomenon, based on post-modern science and technology. There is Global civil war. It is affecting children and women badly. Third wave of feminism is meant to save society, affected by war. Woman is developing with political and economic role in society. Author stands with women in struggle of freedom.

I am not wrong to say that author stands for negation of male authority.

Muhammad Junaid Dhana

War of Slavery

It Changed the History of Humans with change of Narrative

It was the logical result of agriculture and trade. Trade of grains developed market and Mythology. New gods were developed. God of war appeared. It was god of farmers. They needed a war. They needed slaves. They developed god of war. Satins were there to guide the farmers. Agricultural elite had appeared in farmers. They were with large farm and family in the village. They were disliked by majority. They were aggressive in behavior. They were elite as a class. It was class based society in the Neolithic era of agriculture and trade. It appeared by negating the classless society of the hunters. Development of agriculture changed the social narrative. It changed the gender status. It changed the social structure. There was class based behavior and treatment, in Neolithic village. Farmers elite was exploiting class. Satins were standing with elite. They wanted more labor to developed agriculture. Large family labor was felt less than enough. There was space available to enlarge the farm. Labor force was a basic limitation. They thought to collect slaves. Women could not produce labor beyond the limits. She could produce a single baby in a year. Farmers had developed early age marriage tradition to produce more children. It could also work under the limitations. Satins were there. They developed the mind for war. The war of slavery. Farmers developed ideology of war. It was the first war in human history to change social narrative. Farmers army launched war. They attacked the other tribes. They attacked hunters. Farmers declared them "Savage". They called them savage people. They were declared threat to the civilization of farmers. Concept of threat was created. It was popularized. Slogan of war was developed by the farmer elite.

Farmers attacked the tribes to collect slaves. They attacked hunter, fisher and herder tribes. The tribes who were not associated with agriculture. There were tribes who had remained associated with hunting and fishing. Herd rearing tribes and hunters were nomadic in life style. Fishing tribes had developed permanent settlements on the river banks. Herder and hunters were semi-settled. They had been fighting with wild predators. Now they had to fight with human predators. They resisted strongly. They were qualified fighters. However the time and space was favoring the farmers. Independent tribes were losing the war. They were defeated. Farmers were stronger to win the war. Farmers had large population. They had walled villages. They had developed weapon industry. They had surplus grain. Farmers had developed the god of war. They had developed narrative and slogans of war.

They could fight a long war. They had the weapons and potential to win. They wanted slaves. They had developed mind of war. They had developed economy of war. Farmers were funded by traders in war of slavery. Farmers and traders collected slaves. They found unpaid labor. Slaves developed agriculture and trade of the Neolithic era. Women suffered most in the war. Women slaves were used in farm labor and sex labor. Farmers found women to enlarge the family size. A new social structure appeared with war of slavery. Master – slave relation appeared. Slaves had no social rights in the social narrative of slavery. A farmer could keep slave women for sex and labor. Farmers had adopted status of masters. Farmer elite found a large number of slaves. They developed the culture of slavery. Trader also found slaves. Slaves had to provide unpaid labor. They were also a source to produce unpaid labor. Child labor developed in Neolithic culture. Slave family had to work for master. Slave children were providing child labor.

Slavery emerged in Middle East and Fertile Crescent. It spread to South Asia, Middle East and Egypt are found as oldest civilizations of slavery. These are the regions of earliest slavery. Slavery developed into culture in these regions. Slave trade appeared and developed in Egypt and Middle East. Slaves were degraded to the worst in human history. A miserable class structure and relation developed. There was nothing lower in status than slaves. Slaves were changed into a commodity. Woman was affected most. Slave woman was producing children for slave market. Egypt and Iraq have been oldest slave markets. A famous prophet was sold as a child slave in Egypt. He was the prophet Joseph. Joseph was sold to a slave trader. Trader sold him to the slave market of Egypt. Joseph worked as a child slave in Egypt. This has been stated in revealed books. Joseph was son of the prophet Jacob. He was living in the Palestine. Jacob lost his eye sight by weeping. He went blind. Joseph was sold by his brothers. Joseph was eaten by wild wolves. Jacob was told. He went blind by weeping. His son was sold as a slave, he knew. He was father of a child, who was sold as a slave child. There were mothers slave mothers their children were for market. Slave mothers were injured more than Jacob. They were weeping more than Jacob.

Slave Mothers

Slave Mothers Produced Slave Children

Women suffered Neolithic slavery war. They survived torture and exploitation. They tolerated suppression. Women were raped in war of slavery which started almost ten thousand years before Christ (BC). Neolithic ended almost two thousand years before Christ (BC) with role of Iron in technology. Neolithic culture of slavery persisted for 10 thousand years almost. It developed civilization of slavery. Neolithic civilization was based on the narrative of mythology. Neolithic civilization developed class structure and class behavior. It is still working in modern society. Neolithic culture divided humans into master and slave classes. Slave women were like cattle's in social status. They produced slave children. They worked as unpaid laborer. Slave mothers were to produce slave children for the master class. Neolithic agriculture and trade was developed by slaves. Master families produced master class. Slave women produced slave class. Slave mothers supported economy and production in the Neolithic. Slaves were degraded to petty generation. They had no social rights. Master class developed civilization and culture of slavery.

"Priest" was to teach that masters and slaves were natural generation. Slaves were not more than domestic animals. They were traded in slave market. A salve family could be sold in singles. A purchaser could buy all or some members of the slave family. Children were sold in front of mother. Sometimes mother was sold alone. It was unbearable which was tolerated by slave mothers- it was more than heart breaking. Slave mother had no choice. She had to accept the order of master. She could shed tears only without the permission of master. She was injured by soul. However she had to take it as normal. It was tradition. There was nothing to live, but slave mother had to live. She was not allowed to die. Master could not afford suicide. It was loss to masters. It was economic loss of masters –traders in reality. Therefore suicide was not permitted in narrative and tradition. It was presented as a sin. Pieces of the heart were sold. Slave mother survived it. She produced more children for the market. She maintained the generation which was made slave. Slaves were not allowed to live in the town. They were to live in slave colonies out of walled town. Slave mother managed to save language, culture and religion of the slaves. She taught mother language to her children. she taught religion. She made the psychology and behavior of slaves. Slave children were taught by mothers. Slave mother decided to save the generation. She suffered and survived with the hope of good days.

Saint House

Saint was with Narrative of Freedom

First civilization of history appeared in towns. It was middle of the Neolithic era. Neolithic appeared almost ten years before Christ, with beginning of agriculture. Neo-lithic agriculture and trade developed civilization of slavery. Earliest towns have been found almost eight thousand years old. It is almost six thousand years before Christ. Jerusalem was one the Neolithic towns. There were towns in Egypt and Iraq. Syria and Turkey had been regions of Neolithic towns. South Asia had towns on river banks. Indus valley had developed towns such as Harrappa and Mohinjodaro, in Sindh valley. These towns present evidences of Neolithic culture. Slavery appeared with development of agriculture and trade. It was the trade, if we like to decide for single cause of slavery. Agriculture, trade and slavery found origin in Egypt and Middle East. Egypt had developed into super power almost two thousand years before Christ. It had developed into empire. Egypt was the largest market of slaves. Egyptian civilization developed on the river Nile. Neolithic civilization developed on river banks. Neolithic towns had developed in South Asia. There had been river sindh to support the Neolithic agriculture and trade. Slavery was the culture developed in Neolithic. There was saint house, in town. It was under the oak tree in a street of town. It had no rooms and walls. Oak branches worked as roof of the saint house. Saint had a family. It was different than others. There were dogs with saint. There were birds and arboreal animals in the family of saint. Saint was loved by prostitute, slaves and women of the elite class, in the town. Prostitute sang the song of freedom. Saint was poet of freedom. Saint and prostitute, both belonged to slave class. They had achieved freedom. Saint created the songs of freedom. He was negating the narrative of slavery. Narrative of the master class was imposed- saint did not accept it. He did not follow the narrative of master class. He remained unmarried. Saint knew that, he was living in a slave town. He disliked growing a slave family. Saint was not to produce slave children. Saint represented the narrative of freedom. It was recessive in nature. Therefore, narrative of the saint did not contributed in the struggle of freedom. It was not active narrative. Saint presented the ideology of tolerance. He negated violence and aggression. Master class did not resist saint. Masters also accepted the freedom of prostitute. Saint preached the narrative of equality. He presented concept of the all alive. This was concept of freedom. It was the ideology of existentialism, in primitive form. Saint negated the mythology. However the saint was passive and recessive. He was tolerated by the master class.

Saint was not challenge to the status of social structure. He was a person isolated from society. Saint was a sorry face of freedom. He was with a realization of total defeat. He belonged to the tribe, defeated in war of slavery. Saint had realized the fact of slavery. He realized that slavery had been changed into culture. War of slavery had changed the narrative. Slaves had accepted the narrative of slavery. Therefore saint was alone in the town. Prostitute was only friend of the saint with heart and soul. She loved non in the town except the saint. Saint was love in heart of the prostitute. Saint was poet. Prostitute was singer. Poetry of saint was narrative of negation. Saint had sympathies with slaves. He could not help the slaves. He could not oppose the masters. He had adopted the ideology of existence and survival. Saint was not productive. He knew it was unproductive. He was aware with truth of the time and space. Saint was spiritual father of slaves. Saint knew that he could not help slaves. Therefore, he did not help them. Saint was not associated with metaphysics. He was known as the person with super natural potentials. Slaves appeared to believe in concept of metaphysics. Saint was negating the narrative of gods. He was thought a person with close links to gods. He was different from priest. Priest was a servant of master elite. He was representative of gods. priest was to impose narrative of slavery. Which was socio-political narrative of the master class? Saint was not friend of god. He had de-linked from socio-political structure of slavery. He was friend to slaves. Saint was not Enemy of masters. He disliked slavery. He did not dislike any one. He loved humans and animals. Humans and animals were equal in status to saint. He believed all was not creature of the God. God was supreme in the universe. All creatures had divine right of existence and freedom. God had no needs. Saint could feel worries of the animals. He could feel the pains of plants and all others in the world. Shrine of god in the town was religious centre. There was idol of god for worship. Elite class was to impose the narrative of gods. It was slavery. Priest was guardian. He was servant of the king in reality. Saint house was spiritual centre. There was no demand in saint house. It was floor of oak tree. There was nothing in the house except a water pitcher and bowl. There was burning fire. Sometime smock only. Saint was accepted as a requirement by the elite of town. Elite was not concerned about the narrative of equality and freedom. Spiritual feelings of the elite could not be satisfied by the priest and shrine. Women of the elite had many grievances, produced by system and narrative of slavery. Saint house was a spiritual therapy centre for masters and slave class. It was the reason that saint was accepted in the town. Saint and prostitute were slaves, in class origin. They were allowed to live in the town of masters. They were not treated as slaves. Saint and prostitute were only persons with real freedom. They had gained freedom which could not be snatched. Priest disliked the saint and prostitute. It was because priest was guardian of slavery. Saint and prostitute were not to accept it. They were with freedom in the town. Priest was worried. Saint appeared in town of slaves. He was the only voice against slavery. Prostitute was respect and love of saint. Saint and prostitute were not allowed to be buried in graveyard of master class. They were to be buried in the graveyard of slaves. Saints have been there in South Asia and Middle East. There are many shrines of saints in Pakistan, respected by people of all religions.

Prostitute

Prostitute was Salve Girl with real Freedom

She was slave girl beautiful and creative. She learned singing and dancing. She was called prostitute. She was not sex worker. Prostitute adopted art of dancing and singing. It was a profession. Prostitution appeared in Neo-lithic town culture. Town had developed into the market. It was economic and political center. Town was market of the Neolithic trade. Neo-lithic towns developed on river banks. Majority of the agricultural villages had developed on the river banks. Some villages developed into towns. Town was the nucleus of villages. The largest town had developed into capital. Neolithic culture could not grow further, beyond towns. Town could not grow into city. The Neolithic trade could develop towns only. It could not develop city. Therefore Neolithic should be known as era of towns. Town was for elite. It was capital. Town was for trading elite. Farmer elite was holding villages. Prostitution appeared in town culture as a profession. The profession was adopted by slave girls. Towns were constructed by slaves. Oldest towns have been discovered in Egypt, Iraq and South Asia. It is the region of agriculture development. It is region of earliest slavery. Trade appeared and developed in the same region. It is the region – prostitution appeared and developed as a profession. Prostitute was a singer and dancer. She was therefore a professional for entertainment of the elite. She was a professional for romance and entertainment.

There was environment and resources of art development in the town. Political and economical elite was there. King was there in the capital town. It was the kingdom of agricultural elite. It was a small kingdom. The Neolithic kingdom could not expand to large region. The capital was with palace of the king. The officials were appointed by the king. Tribal chief had grown to the king. Kingdom appeared and developed in Egypt, Iraq and South Asia. Capital town was center of political elite, economical elite and religious elite. Largest Temple was there in the capital town. Chief god was there. King and god were close to each others. Master elite was polygamous. Wife was not prostitute. She could not be. She could not sing. She could not dance like a prostitute. She was to produce children for husband. There were wives many for a husband. Elite wanted entertainment. Prostitute provided. There was a space for prostitute. She appeared. Women of the master class could not adopt prostitution. She was not allowed. she was under custody as a wife. Slave girl could adopt prostitution. Prostitute was the slave daughter. Elite daughters were to dance for the god. Woman of the elite could dance to entertain the god.

There were festivals and dancing days – specified. There were dancing festivals. There were celebrations of elite. Slave woman was not allowed to dance for god. It was god of the elite. Prostitute could sing and dance for elite. She did it. Elite woman was to dance for god. Elite class needed to please the god. Unhappy god could not be afforded. god had major role to play in the narrative of mythology. Happiness of the god was essential. Neolithic culture was based on the religious narrative. Master elite had developed customs-pleasing for god. Elite woman was to dance for entertainment of god. Prostitution was a philosophy of freedom. It was interesting. Prostitute was not slave. She found freedom in prostitution. She was not owned by any one. She was common to all. She could be taken as personal keep by a lord. However commonly, she was not liked as housewife. Prostitute disliked being a traditional wife. She was at freedom as prostitute. She could not like to lose her social freedom - she enjoyed freedom and art. Prostitute developed the art of music. Poet, musician and prostitute were associated. All were slaves. Prostitute was bound to a specific street in the town. Prostitute house was enlightened at night. She had a decorated house. She was love of the elite. Prostitute was a prosperous woman. She was financed by the elite. She was not poor. She was not slave. Prostitute had developed economic friendship with elite. She danced – she sang for elite. She was liked and loved for entertainment. Prostitute was aware of the reality. There was freedom in prostitution. It developed in the culture of slavery. Prostitute was only woman with social freedom in the state of slavery. Prostitute developed freedom in the culture of slavery. It was creativity. She created the space for freedom. Prostitute achieved freedom in the civilization of slavery. Prostitute regained the woman had lost in the war of slavery. Religious elite was contradictory opponent of prostitution. They called it sin and crime. Elite woman was Jealous on the freedom of prostitute. Priest was unhappy.

Veil

Veil is fear of male

It was imposed by the trading class, in Neo-lithic towns.

Veil is a character of the classical narrative. It is not religious wear-in Origin-It was developed by the classical traders, in neolithic towns. The veil is associated with Islamic social values. It is total misunderstanding. Veil is social behavior adopted from the civilization of slavery. Veil was imposed on women by trading class. Traders made woman-the domestic and indoor animal in humans. Social evolution stands with logic. Woman was domesticated and veiled by trader families of the Neolithic civilization, almost six thousand years before Christ (BC).

No one, other, should see the face of my wife. It was logic behind the veil of woman. Woman could not step out of the threshold. She was imprisoned behind house walls. She was to hide her face-if she had to go out of house. She could not step out alone. It was the morality for women, developed by traders. They had to travel from town to town. They were bound to remain out of house for months. They had slave girls with them. Wife was to stay at home. Traders imposed veil and indoor confinement on wife. It was not a problem with farmers. Therefore, farmer did not impose veil and house confinement on wife. Veil was made as basic value of religion in Islam by traders. However, it was not accepted by the woman, other than trading class. House confinement has elapsed and veil covering is working in countries with classical Social narrative. It is imposed on women in Saudi Arabia. The veil for woman and condition of indoor living is not Arabian in origin. Most of the Arab tribes were nomads of desert before Islam. They were idol worshiping in religion. Each tribe of Arabia had a "god". Idol of the god was placed in house of God at Macca. There were 360 idols. Macca was town of trader tribes. There were some tribes associated with agriculture. There was limited land for agriculture in desert of Arabia. Tribes with agriculture had adopted Christianity. The woman was not veiled by farmers. Woman was participant in farming. Therefore, she could not observe veil. She was working woman. Nomads were herd rearing tribes. They had herds of goat, sheep and cattle. Woman of herding tribe was also a working woman. She was not observing veil. Macca was town of traders. Woman was not working-in traders family. She was to live indoor and observe veil. The tradition was basically developed by traders. Working women has never observed veil in the history of social evolution. The veil was introduced and imposed by traders. They demanded indoor confinement of women. They proposed veil to cover body and face. Veil appeared as a class character. It was not a religious value. Islamic narrative was developed in Macca. Veil was included in the narrative. It was presented as a basic value for Muslim. A slave woman could not wear Burka in Arabs. It was imposed in the Regions- conquered by Arabs. Muslim rulers were not interested to impose veil on women. However, the Muslim priest was most interested-in veil and indoor limitations of women. Woman was not working woman in priest family. The Muslim priest was earning from religious services. Priest was to preach for veil and indoor life for women. He was left unnoticed by the working family. South Asia suffered slavery. It developed into classical slavery before the crackdown of Areans from central Asia. There are different trends about the veil and the woman in South Asia. It provides logic of veil and indoor confinement of women. The veil was developed as religious value by traders and priest. We find living evidences in south Asia of present day. Woman has never accepted indoor confinement and veil in south Asia. Priest is always angry on this behavior of women. Women do not care. South Asia of present day is semi-modern in social status. It has passed through slavery and classical narrative. Woman has never liked to live as indoor animal. She has not adopted veil as a divine order. It is very much evident in the social behavior of women-in South Asia. Women of the farming community do not observe veil. She was never bound to indoor enclosure. Farmers in Pakistan are classical in behavior and narrative. Farmer family is part of working class. Woman is participant in production system. Woman works more than man in farmer family. She is to manage domestic necessities. Cooking, cleaning and washing are responsibility of woman. She is responsible for feeding the family. Farmer woman stands with major role in farm production and family management. She is working woman. She cannot hide behind veil. She does not need it. She is nucleus of family. However, she is under social rules developed by the classical narrative. Man is owner of the farm. He is owner of family. He is the owner of the wife and children. Rights of ownership make him king of family. Women is working subordinate. She is servant of the husband. She is taught to be servant. There is a tribe in Pakistan. They are kiln workers. People are property less. They do not have even houses to live. Kiln worker families live at kiln colonies. They are slave colonies in society. The people are slave in society. The people are slave in social treatment. It is called bound labor. The kiln families work for making and baking bricks at the kiln. Kiln owners belong to the elite class. Kiln workers remain houseless in life. They receive advance money from kiln owner. The labor is bought on minimum vages. They cannot meet the necessities, even with lowest living standard. They stand in need of loan to meet the expenditures. Laws and rules favor kiln owners. Kiln workers are slaves in social status. Woman works. Children also work to provide bonded labor.

Woman Is responsible member to meet the requirements. She works more than man. The woman is not with veil. She cannot do it. She cannot afford veil. She finds less money to wear clothes. There are rules and laws-in Pakistan-against bonded labor. It is only paper work. The kiln worker families are professional in making and baking bricks.

There are herd rearing tribes in Pakistan. Tribes of Balochistan a province of Pakistan-were herding tribes-in origin. The region is not suitable for agriculture. It consists of dry-arid region-with arid plains and dry mountains. Baloch tribes are Areans who settled in the region almost two thousand years before Christ. However, archaeology presents evidences of pre-Arean civilization in Baluchistan. Balochistan has been the region of herd-rearing tribes. Baloch woman was working woman. She was grazing goat-sheep herds in the plains and mountains. She was not veil wearing. Towns developed in Balochistan almost eight thousand years BC. Town was market of animals and handicrafts. Areans demolished pre-Arean Balochistan. Herd-rearing Arean tribes settled in the region. The Balochistan has been tribal region in history. Woman of the chief family were to observe veil. He had fort house in center of the town. A woman of tribal elite was also bound in veil. Majority population belonged to working class. Woman of the working class has never observed Perdah. Baloch tribes are secular in social behavior and attitude. Woman is hard working subordinate in the family. She is property of male as wife and daughter.

Northern region of Pakistan is veil area. The population is with tribal culture. Tribes are with trade economy. Northern mountains are green with rivers and springs. Some tribes are herd rearing. The region produces a large variety of fruits. There are fertile plains in frontier province of Pakistan. Northern autonomous agencies are mountainous and rocky in topography. The tribes have been traders. Woman is to live in veil under male domination. Woman is not allowed to step out of house. Woman is not working member of family. She is bound to live indoor life. Woman education is not permitted. Malala Yousaf Zai was attacked by tribal militants. She was working for woman education. North and Pakhtoon region of Pakistan is veil area. Afghanistan is also veil region. Tribal culture of the region is based on classical narrative. Woman is social slave in reality. Tribes have been associated with trade economy. Modern economy has not developed in Afghanistan and tribal north of Pakistan. Taliban were fighting to establish a classical empire. They are still fighting against modernism. They do not like education and freedom of women. Islamic militants are fighting against modernism. They believe in narrative of classical civilization. There is another tribe in south Asia. They are hunters. They live in kinship family groups. They are living with culture of hunters. They represent living fossils of hunting tribes. Tribe is nomadic in living style. They live in cloth tents. A group pitches tents out of a village. Male hunt all type of wild animals in the region. They use iron weapons for hunting. Spears and axes are common weapons. They follow the prey with hunting dogs. Woman and children are participant in hunting. There Is no concept of veil. They have sexual freedom. Woman is not social slave. New generations of the tribe are adopting settlement.

There is another tribe of nomads in south Asia. They rear cattle herds. They move from place to another with change in season. They represent living fossils of herd rearing culture of prehistory. There are other people in south Asia. They are different and interesting people. They are nomads in living style. They live in tent villages near cities. Woman is working and managing in family. Woman is head of family. Woman is with authority to decide the disputes. They are not part of state laws and rules. Woman is beggars. Women begin city. Male is only sexual member of family. Woman stands with social authority. Therefore she does not need to stand under veil. Veil is fear of male in reality.

Song of Tragedy

Slave Woman Created Literature of Tragedy

It was the song of tragedy which developed into literature of slavery. Literature of tragedy appeared in slavery. Slavery was the worst tragedy in social history. Song of tragedy was created by the broken heart. It was heart of the slave mother. She was helpless mother. Tragedy emerged in war of slavery. It developed in the culture of slavery. Slaves created songs of tragedy. It was the expression of sorrow. It was the pray to god. Slaves were lower to the animal status. They were a trade commodity. Culture of slave trade affected the slave family. Slave family was nothing more than a cattle family. It was the degradation of human unobserved in human history. Slave market appeared. Children of the slave family were for market. Think about a slave family for sale. One was there to buy a child. Mother was not allowed to raise objection on the sale of her children. It was a moment very much injuring-husband, children and women (the mother) were sold. They were purchased by different people. They could be purchased by traders. They could be purchased by lords. Slaves were sold and purchased like animals in market. Slaves were not animals. They were humans. They had human heart and soul. Mother created the song of tragedy. Woman was first poetess of tragedy. She created a pray song for her children separated by traders. Salve mother was first tragedy poetess. She was first tragedy singer. Song of tragedy appeared in Neo-lithic slavery.

Meso-lithic was era of freedom. Mesolithic tribes had developed social freedom. A woman was in social authority. Mother was honored in Mesolithic tribe. Mesolithic was with culture of peace, honor and love. Causes of dispute were not there. Woman was managing the family. Man was working partner. Mesolithic had developed culture of sharing and cooperation. They had developed the ways to live with nature. Woman was creative. Male was productive in behavior and psychology. They had developed culture of freedom and pleasure. They had created songs of joy and pleasure. They celebrated the big success in hunting. They celebrated the successful hunting of large animals. They celebrated the change in season. They celebrated the birth of child. They celebrated marriage. Fishing and herd rearing tribes had their own festivals and celebrations. They had developed gods, according to their life style. They had the customs of worship. Woman was to decide for her Marriage. Woman had right of choice. She enjoyed social freedom and authority, in Meso-lithic culture. Some anthropologists point to the tradition of polyandry in Mesolithic culture. However, there is no convincing reason to support the concept of polyandry. It was not needed. A woman was with freedom of love and marriage. She had the freedom of choice. She could change her love. She could change spouse. She was not in need of polyandry. Mesolithic had developed a social culture and morality. Morality was based on mythology.

Love was no crime. Mesolithic people were not aware of social discrimination. Mesolithic tribes had manufactured drum and flute. They had developed music. They enjoyed dance in celebrations. Women had ornaments to wear in celebrations. Males were also with ornaments. Mesolithic people were living with love and pleasure. They had songs of joy and happiness. They had created the culture of love songs and dances. They were not to face any social tragedy. There were some natural problems with them. Major cause of sadness was death. Hunters could be killed by predators. Children could be easy prey. Such events could be cause of sorrow and sadness. There was natural death. They had associated death and casualties with super natural forces. Maso-lithic people had tragedy free culture. They had to suffer natural problems. Diseases and disasters were taken as anger and punishment of gods.

Social tragedy appeared in the Neolithic slavery. Causes were based on trade and agriculture. Neolithic developed worst of the human history. Aggression, torture, discrimination and culture of exploitation was new to humans. Neolithic developed culture of slavery. Slavery changed social structure and behavior. Freedom, peace, love, sharing and cooperation was lost. Exploitation, aggression and slavery are there with us. Classical and modern tragedy is prominent in modern society. Literature of tragedy represents social problems, in modern society. Classical Poetry is deep rooted in tragedy. Psychology and behavior of the people indicates inheritance of the social syndromes. Social behavior, based on mythology and slavery is found deep rooted is South Asia.

Sarah

Sara was working for freedom

Sara was wife of Ibrahim. She was mother of classical religions. Ibrahim migrated to Egypt from Iraq. It was almost 3 thousand years before Christ (BC). Ibrahim was known as father of classical religions. Classical religions are Judaism, Christianity and Islam. The religions appeared in the civilization of classical slavery. It was the age of iron technology. Classical religions challenged mythology of Neo-lithic culture. Ibrahim challenged the culture of Neolithic slavery in Iraq. He was sentenced punishment by the king of Iraq. Ibrahim was sentenced death by burning alive. He escaped. Ibrahim migrated to Egypt with his followers. It was almost 3 thousand years (BC). Ibrahim introduced the God in Iraq. He negated Mythology and presented Antislavery narrative. King of Iraq and his Cabinet decided to burn Ibrahim alive. Master could punish slaves. They could burn them alive. It was right with masters. Narrative of slavery allowed it. Ibrahim fled to Egypt. Egypt was another Kingdom of slavery. Ibrahim and followers were arrested by a tribal chief in Egypt. They were imprisoned. The story of Ibrahim has been stated in religious books. Sara, wife of Ibrahim, was liked and chased by chief, as it is stated. He thought to keep Sara. Chief asked Ibrahim about his relation with Sara. Ibrahim told that she was his sister. Chief released all the followers of Ibrahim after some days. He allowed Ibrahim to live in the region. Chief gifted him land for agriculture. He gifted a slave girl to Sara. She was Hajra to serve the Sara. Sara was not touched by the Tribal chief. He tried many times, but failed. He could not succeed, because God was there to protect the honor of Sara. Ibrahim was doubtful about Sara. God assured him that Sara was protected by God. There is a similar story in Indian mythology. It is about Seete and Ram.

Ibrahim settled there in Egypt, with kindness of the Chief. He cultivated the land and reared cattles. He appeared as a prosperous farmer. Ibrahim had a herd of cattles and fertile land. He found wealth and pleasure in Palestine with help of the local chief. Chief was kind to Ibrahim and Sara. He had gifted a slave girl to serve Sara. She was Hajra. Ibrahim married Hajra. Sara disliked this marriage. Sara was dominant woman. Hajra was separated with her newly born son. She was departed from the family. Ibrahim left her at Macca near a spring of sweet water. Macca was a small town of traders. Sara gave birth to a son. He was Izhaq. Ibrahim and disciples was a small population. The group believed in monism. They planted monism in Palestine. This small group of Ibrahim family and disciples developed into a population. With belief in monism. They appeared as Jews in the region. Sara family developed monism. The family was respected in Jews as a spiritual family. Sara was mother of Prophets. The family developed classical religions in the regions. It was struggle of freedom against classical slavery. The struggle was planted and developed by the Sara and family. Hajra settled out of town the Mecca with her son.He was Ismaile.

The Royal Slave

He was Son of Prophet who was Sold by his Brother

Joseph was sold as a slave. Brothers sold him to a slave trader. The slave trader was going to Egypt for marketing. It was the largest market of slaves. Egypt was a kingdom under rule of pharaohs. It was a Neolithic Kingdom. Agriculture and trade had been developed. There was demand of slave labor in Egypt. Egypt was largest slave market in Nile Valley. Joseph was sold to a salve trader. He was going to Egypt for sale of his salves. He was passing through Kanaan. It was the region of Israelites. Joseph was from family of Sara. He was son of the prophet Jacob. Joseph was very beautiful boy. Brothers sold Joseph to the slave trader who met them on the road to Egypt. Jacob asked his sons about Joseph. He was eaten by desert wolves. They told to the father. Desert wolves could attack goat and people. It was not unusual. Joseph brothers presented clothes to the father, soaked in blood of goat. Jacob had found it by heart. It was not truth. Jacob went to the desert. He called desert wolves. Wolves appeared in front of Jacob. He asked wolves about Joseph. They had never attacked on goat of Jacob family. They were blamed to hide the truth. Wolves told the

Jacob. Joseph was killed or sold by the brothers. Jacob had found the reality. He could not punish his sons. It was result of family contradictions. Joseph was heat of Jacob. The family had spiritual status in Israelites. Joseph could be next prophet. Joseph brothers were caught in gealousy. There was tradition of slavery, which made joseph a slave for market. He belonged to Sara family. The family was Royal in spiritual and economic terms. Joseph was very beautiful and creative boy. He had unmatched personality. Story of Joseph has been stated in book of genesis. Jacob loved Joseph very much. He was most dear to Jacob. It developed jealousy against Joseph. Joseph could be appointed spiritual head of Israelites. It was most probable. Joseph brothers were right to feel. They sold him to slave market. Jacob wept a lot on the loss of his beloved son. He lost his eye sight. He could not forget Joseph. Jacob was weeping most of time. He became weak, sick and blind. Joseph was sold in the slave market of Egypt. He was brilliant, beautiful boy. Joseph was bought by a woman of elite. Joseph belonged to a royal and spiritual family. He grew into an intelligent, creative and attractive young man. Joseph could translate and explain the massage of dreams. It is stated in book genesis. There was other in Cairo. Joseph was very exact in explaining dreams. The woman who bought Joseph fell in love with him. It is very nice story of romance. Romance of a woman of elite, with a slave. She was wife of minister in Egypt. She was young and beautiful. She felt her slave and lost heart. She liked to share bed with her slave, the Joseph. Joseph avoided. The woman was angry. Anger changed in to revenge. Ultimately, she accused Joseph. She registered a complaint, Joseph had committed sexual assault. She claimed. Joseph was sex criminal. Case was heard by jury. Jury decided in favor of the slave. Joseph was released from prison. There are interesting questions radiating in the story. A jury was deciding the disputes between people. It was Egypt under pharaohs about three thousand years (BC). Slaves had rights in law. Trial of Joseph indicates, there was justice. Jury listened arguments of Joseph and decided in favor of a slave. It was a judiciary in civilization of slavery, under the Pharaoh. A slave could get justice. He could win his case against an opponent of elite. Decision of Joseph trial stands as an evidence. Judiciary system of pharaohs was the best found in history. I may wish, that much justice in Pakistan. I may not expect. Judiciary system of the modern civilization is many folds less in comparison. An advocate may mold and remold the truth in modern court. I dislike slavery. I like pharaohs for only reason. Judiciary was independent. A slave could rely on court of pharaoh. I cannot expect in Pakistan. I am sorry. We the poor's are less than slaves of Egypt. I feel it very much true. Slaves of Egypt enjoyed much more freedom of mind and heart. They enjoyed human rights more than poor class in Pakistan. They were slaves. We are less than salves. Joseph was made a minister in pharaoh regime. He was appointed as minister of agriculture. A slave of potential was not ignored by pharaoh. A feminine is reported to affect the region. It lasted for a decade almost. Egypt produced enough grain to feed the population of region. It was due to the management of Joseph in agriculture. Joseph brothers went to Egypt for grain. They found, Joseph was a minister there in Egypt. They told to Jacob the blind. He visited Egypt. He met with Joseph and pharaoh. Jacob praised and prayed for pharaoh. Israelites migrated to Egypt in majority. They were accommodated.

Crisis of Iron Technologies

Development of Iron Technology changed Economy and Politics Negating Stone Technology

Neolithic culture had developed on the basis of refined stone tools. Development of agriculture had basic importance. Agriculture was new mean of production. It brought a big change. It changed economy, culture, narrative and social structure. Neolithic narrative appeared opposite to the previous one. Neo-lithic slavery had negated the culture of social freedom. Neo-lithic was negated by Iron technology It destabilized the social structure. It worked as basic factor for change. It challenged the narrative of Neo-lithic slavery. A new crisis appeared with development of Iron technology.

Emergence of the new technology produces a social mutation. It develops a social group which differs from general population. It appears as a quantitative change in the population. Iron technology did the same. Iron technology developed in Middle East. It has been stated in religious books. King David has been stated as an expert in iron technology. David, the Prophet, was first king of Jews in Middle East. He played an important role in development of iron technology. Almost thousand years before Christ (BC), Jews had established a capital city. It was Jerusalem

Iron technology replaced stone tools and weapons. Population with iron technology appeared strong in tools and weapons. Population associated with stone tools could not complete iron technology. Iron technology appeared with revolutionary potential. Iron tools were sharp, strong, effective and efficient. Iron technology was welcomed as gift of nature by farmers. Iron industry developed in towns. There was demand of iron tools and weapons. It developed iron industry. Farmers adopted iron tools to increase agri- production. They enlarged their farms. Iron technology played revolutionary role in development of economy. Trade economy progressed as a result of increase in agri-production. This was a social mutation. It produced a new social group in population of stone technology. Kingdom with iron technology developed army with iron weapons. It was swift and strong army. Social mutation justified the unjustified war. A new crisis erupted. Farmers were persuaded to join the army. Slaves were also made soldiers in this army. King wanted to expand kingdom. Neolithic culture was challenged. Farmers army launched the war. A new narrative was developed. It was based on negation of Neolithic narrative. Importance of the iron technology was recognized. Many tribes adopted iron technology. Other remained associated with old stone tools. They were defeated easily by the army with iron weapons. The towns were attacked and defeated by the armies with iron weapons.

Kingdom expanded to large area. Large kingdoms were developed. It was the war of elite. Farmers were providing soldiers. Traders were funding the war against stone culture. A war is always based on social contradictions, based on economic contradictions. A basic contradiction had appeared between iron and stone technology. It was cause of the war. Neolithic towns were attacked and conquered by the army with iron weapons. The war developed into a large scale crisis. It was new upset. The people with stone tools resisted the attacks. However, they were not successful. They were defeated. Old towns were defeated and demolished. It was a new war of slavery. Independent tribes were conquered and made slave. Iron technology established the civilization of slavery. Large kingdoms developed as a result of iron technology. Town developed into large city. Agriculture progressed. Trade economy developed manifold. Narrative of slavery found strength. Oldest large kingdoms and cities developed in Egypt, Middle East and south Asia. It provides with physical evidences of the war in the region.

Women were badly affected again. Women were target of soldiers. There was a big change in behavior of soldiers. The slave women were not target. Women of the master elite suffered this war. It was the war of elite. Therefore slave women were not much affected. Iron army conquered towns. Soldiers killed, raped and tortured the women of elite. They made them slave wives. Slaves participated in this war as soldiers

Slave woman was not much worried. Soldiers of iron army were not interested in slave women. They were interested in elite women. They were interested in wealth and gold. Generals had heart for women in the palace of king. Soldiers selected other beautiful women. Slaves were not killed. They were required by the new masters. There was a second mutation in war. The importance of this mutation was not noticed and considered by the master elite. It was the inclusion of slaves in army. Slaves were taken in army to meet the shortage of man power. Slaves were armored with iron weapons. They found a soldier behavior and attitude. Slave soldiers had learned to fight with weapons. They found the chance to attack and kill the masters in opponent army. Slaves in the iron army were successful soldiers. Large armies of the great kings had strong group of slave soldiers. Now the slaves were not as weak and defeated as they were in the stone culture of Neolithic. Now the slave women was not only producing slaves for trade and agriculture. She was also producing soldiers. It was very much important social mutation. It produced an armored group of slaves. They were taking experience of war. This mutation worked in the antislavery wars. Iron technology changed the socio-political structure. Iron technology developed agriculture and trade. Large cities developed to rule the towns and villages. Large kingdoms and powerful kings appeared, with large armies. Slavery was more established. Iron technology laid foundation of anti-slavery wars.

Suicide of Cleopatra

Cleopatra was fighting for Freedom with weapon her Beauty

She was Queen of Egypt. Cleopatra was Greek in blood and figure. She belonged to family of Ptolemy-a general in army of Alexander-the great. Ptolemy established rule over Egypt-after death of the Alexander. Egypt was conquered by Greek army in 332 BC. Cleopatra was Queen when Romans attacked Egypt. She was a beautiful genius woman. She was an intelligent ruler. Cleopatra was a peace loving and kind Queen of Egypt. Cleopatra of Egypt was not dethroned like Saba of the Yemen. Queen Saba surrendered to the king Suleman. Queen of Egypt did not surrender. She committed suicide after defeat. Roman emperor Octavian attacked Egypt of Cleopatra. It was 31 years BC. Octavian had taken over Roman throne. He attacked to include Egypt in the Roman Empire. Cleopatra resisted. She fought. She lost. She committed suicide. Cleopatra was last in family Ptolemy. Ptolemy established his rule on Egypt in 323 BC after the death of Alexander-the great. Egypt had been super power in region under rule of Pharaohs. Egypt of Pharaohs had developed agriculture. It was largest state of slavery on the river Nile. Pharaohs had established political and economic control over the region. However, they had lost. Ptolemy became ruler of Egypt as a general of Greece army. He established his sovereignty as a king of Egypt. Ptolemy family ruled Egypt for almost 300 years. Ptolemy had shifted capital to Alexandria. It was a new city established after name of Alexander. Alexandria had developed into centre of research and education. It was made a city of knowledge by Ptolemy. He was himself great scholar. Greece science, philosophy and culture were taught in the schools of Alexandria. Alexandria was made a city of schools by the Ptolemy. There were schools with scholars of different sciences. Alexandria was city of education. Natural sciences, medicine, astronomy and social sciences were developed in schools of Alexandria. Students and scholars from different regions had gathered in Alexandria. Arab and Indian students were there in Alexandria. Alexandria was made a prosperous city. It developed as a center of culture and education. Ptolemy dynasty developed agriculture and trade economy. Egypt developed into a peaceful prosperous state in the rule of Ptolemy family. Rulers adopted title of Pharaoh. Cleopatra was the last Pharaoh in the Ptolemy dynasty. She was a beautiful and genius queen of Egypt. She was loved by farmers and slaves in Egypt. Roman Empire was in chaos after the rebellion of slaves. Greece elite was in civil war. Senate had lost controls. Republic was paralysed. Julius Caesar was a powerful general in Greece army. He was fighting for the Greece Empire. Caesar returned to Rome in 49 BC. Slave population of Rome welcomed Caesar. Rome-the capital of empire had developed into city of characterless elite. Senators were interested in corruption. Master slave relationship had gone contaminated with corruption. The elite class of Rome was unconcerned. Rome was a rich city. Roman had collected slaves from conquered region of the empire. Senators were living luxury life. Farmers, workers and slaves in Rome had no food to eat. There was much grain. It was not for slaves. Elite was angry and revengeful. They were punishing slaves. Slaves had killed elite families in the war of freedom. Slave rebellion was unforgettable for the Roman elite. Slave protested against senate when Caesar returned to Rome. It was 49 before the Christ, almost thirty years after the slave rebellion against slavery. Senate had been cruel and revengeful to slaves. Senators had lost trust and support of farmers and slaves. Caesar had observed. Senate had failed to control the empire. The empire was going to disintegrate. Civil war was accelerating. A new rebellion of slaves could be fatal. Caesar seized political powers. Senate was not in position to resist the seizer of political power. Caesar suspended political narrative of the republic. He imposed dictatorship. Caesar took over as an emperor. He was first emperor of the Roman Empire 49 before Christ. Caesar consolidated the empire. Dictatorship of corruption had failed. Dictatorship of justice succeeds. Caesar appeared as successful emperor.

Caesar eradicated anti-empire elements. He established peace which lasted for almost two centuries. This is known as period of "Roman Peace". Caesar attacked Egypt of Cleopatra. Cleopatra avoided war with a strong Roman army. She managed a meeting with Caesar. She was a woman with heart, brain and beauty. Caesar was a general with heart, muscles and sword. Cleopatra succeeded in war of love. Caesar lost and surrendered. Cleopatra succeeded to avoid the war. She saved her slaves, farmers and elite class. Egypt could not resist the Roman army. She was aware of the fact. She thought to avoid war. Cleopatra was the queen who was kind to her people. She was a kind and intelligent lady. She saved her people from the swords of a strong army. Cleopatra developed romantic friendship with Caesar. She married and gave birth to a son by Caesar in 47 BC. He was named Caesarion. Caesar returned to Rome in 47 BC. He was assassinated in Rome. It was a struggle of power between the senate of republic and emperor. Civil war restarted after the assassination of Caesar. Rebels were defeated by Marc Antony and Octavian. They were generals from Caesar family. One was adopted son of Caesar. The other was step-nephew. They collaborated and coordinated the war against rebels. Senate failed to restore republic. Antony and Octavian succeed to establish control over the empire 42 BC. It was again problem for Cleopatra. Marc Antony was made governor of eastern empire. He appeared as a new threat to the independence of Egypt. Cleopatra was to avoid the war with empire once again. She planned to meet Antony. She managed it. Cleopatra developed friendship with Antony. Friendship developed into love. Beauty of Cleopatra changed war into love. Antony did not attack Egypt. He accepted rule of the queen on Egypt. Love of Antony and Cleopatra developed peace and friendship with Egypt. Cleopatra married Antony in 41 BC. It was disliked by Octavian. He wanted to conquer Egypt. He wanted to include fertile land of Egypt in Roman Empire. Octavian attacked on Egypt in 31 BC. Antony supported Cleopatra. It was the war in sea. Roman Empire had developed a strong marine army. They had established control over sea. Cleopatra and Antony fought together against the army of empire. They lost. They did not like to be under arrest. Cleopatra and Antony committed suicide. They were buried side by side. It was sign of classical love. Cleopatra avoided war twice to save her people.

Mary Was There

Saint Mary had developed Narrative of Christianity Negating Mythology

Roman Empire was new chapter of the Greece Empire. Romans established and developed narrative of slavery. They adopted technology developed by Greece. Roman also acquired ideology of Greeks. They had developed a strong army equipped with iron weapons. Roman Empire was founded on disintegrate of Greeks Empire. Alexander the great had established Greece Empire by defeating Iran. Greeks were superior in science and technology. They had a number of scholars. Real power with Greeks was advancement in science, technology and philosophy. Aristotle was king of Greeks ideology. Alexander the Great was unprecedented commander of war. The Greece army equipped with latest war technology and strategy. Alexander defeated Iran with pleasing success. Alexander died in 323. He was buried in Mesopotemia. Alexander died at the age of 33. He had no family heir of the empire. Alexander had established. Greeks had not developed any institution with rights to transfer political power. Death of the Alexander appeared or rotten had of fish. It caused disintegration of the Empire. There was not central binding force available. Empire disintegrated. Ptolemy a famous scholar found Egypt as a share. Army generals divided the conquered Empire. Greece Empire had been divided into generals of Alexander army. They had established regional government. Rome was developing in this period as s city state. Rome was developing in trade and technology. Romans had developed a strong army. It was right time for the Romans. They attacked on disintegrating empire. They were advancing successfully. Defeating Greece generals. Jupiter was gathering power. Xeus was losing war. Romans had established senate in the Rome. Senate was elected body of Roman elite. They were establishing Roman republic. Roman had adopted ideology of Plato to establish the Roman republic. Senate of Rome was elected according to the ideology of Plato. Romans had senate of elected members. It was to elect the king of republic. Roman had succeed to replace Xeus with Jupiter. They had taken over the Greece empire. Romans developed largest empire around the Mediterranean Sea. Rome appeared as the largest rich city of the world. It was the capital of the super power. Roman Empire had extended to Asia and Africa. Europe was included in the empire. Empire was run as a republic. It was rule of master elite. Senate of the republic had established control one hundred years before Christ (BC). It worked until four hundred years after Christ (AD). Roman Empire is known to rule for 500 years. Empire disintegrated almost 400 years after Christ (AD). Senate failed. Rule of master elite was opposed and resisted. A different social experience appeared in Roman Empire. It was movement of freedom. Rebellions of slaves were real wound to the empire. It was 70 years before Christ (BC). Slave army attacked on the empire. Slaves had found iron weapons. They were soldiers. They had learned to fight wars. Slaves were gladiators. Gladiators were brave fighters. They were slaves in status. Anti-slavery war was real story in Roman Empire. Slaves succeeded to win the war. Roman Empire was climax of slavery. Slaves army challenged the narrative of slavery. It was the great revolution in history. Jupiter was attacked. Spartacas attacked. He was a gladiator. He organized the slave army. Commanded the slave army in war of freedom. Women participated in the war. Women played a significant role. They encouraged slave population to fight for freedom. Slave women contributed. They scarified. Women played active role in organization of freedom fighters. Slaves had been fighting for masters-for benefit of masters-on order of master. They picked up sword against the masters-against slavery. It was a big change. It was a great revolution. Slave mother was there to fight and to help his fighting son. It was a war of weapons and ideology. Slaves were defeated in armed struggle. Romans lost ideology. Romans were standing with the history. Slave changed the history. Spartacas was arrested and hanged. He had hanged the Empire of slavery. Senate was paralysed. A successful general Julius Caesar took over as emperor in 49 BC. Republic had died. Senators killed the emperor in 44 BC. Step son of Caesar-Octavian recaptured throne in 31 BC. They re-imposed slavery.

Jesus Christ took birth after Spartacas. He was an unusual birth. Mary was great mother. Jesus Christ was prophet of slave. He was crucified to control the movement of freedom. Jesus attacked on narrative of slavery. Mary was there to fight for Christianity. Jupiter was defeated.

Mary-Mother of Freedom

Mary was first in History with Narrative Freedom after War of Slavery

Jesus Christ was born 30 years after suicide of the Cleopatra. Suicide of Cleopatra was protest of a woman against slavery. Cleopatra was Queen of Egypt and Queen of beauty. She married with the generals to save Egypt. At last, King of Rome attacked Egypt of Queen. She fought. She lost. She committed suicide. Cleopatra protested against slavery of Romans. Octavian defeated Cleopatra. Elite of Egypt was made slave. It was 30 years before Christ. 70 years before Christ (BC)-great freedom fighter-Spartacas was killed by Romans-in war against slavery. Birth of the Jesus was birth of the freedom. Mary was mother of freedom. Jesus fought for freedom. He won the war. Jesus was great genius. He changed history. Greatest miracle of Jesus was negation of Roman mythology. He negated the narrative of slavery. Jesus negated the Jupiter and developed narrative of freedom. He was prophet of slaves. Jesus was son of great mother. Christianity was great revolution in social history of human. The revolution of freedom was planted and watered by Mary.

Mary was daughter of slaves. She was born in a religious family. She was almost 13 years at the birth of Jesus. Mary was a saint lady in blooming youth. She was born in Nazareth-a town of Galilee. Galilee was area of agriculture. It was a province of farmers. Yusaf, her husband, was a carpenter. He was to prepare agricultural tools for farmers. Family was Jew in religion. Local farmers were followers of the same religion. The population of Galilee was slave of Romans. Jesus was a slave by birth. He was born in a slave family of Galilee. Population of Galilee was slave of Romans. Population was slave by generations. Iran and Greece had ruled as masters before Romans occupied Galilee. It was a slave region in history. Slave culture was deep routed way of life. Jews were farmers, traders and labourers. Trade Jews had been part of Elite. However, Romans were masters. Jews had lost freedom when Iran occupied the region. They had adopted welcome attitude for masters. Jew elite were partner with Roman elite. They had accepted Romans as masters. Zikria was priest in Jerusalem. Mary was relative of the Zikria. She was educated in Jerusalem. She obtained education of religion, classical philosophy and mathematics. Joseph met her in Jerusalem. Joseph used to present flowers to Mary-as stated in gospels. Mary was always glad to see Joseph with flowers. She returned to Nazareth-in Galilee-after completing her education. She was betrothed with Joseph, who was living in Bethlehem-a town in Galilee. Mary was 13 years when married with Joseph. Jesus was different. He was asexual birth of Mary. Jesus was a miraculous birth. Mary was pregnant. It was spiritual. She was told about it by the angel Gabrile. Angel Gabrile appeared to inform Mary about the spiritual pregnancy. She was going to be pregnant without sex. She was told by the angel Gabrile. It was unusual. Angel Gabrile had met and talked to only woman in history. She was Mary. The event is stated by Mathew and Luke. Holy Quran-the revealed book of Muslim states that Mary was holy mother. Holy Quran supports Mathew and Luke. Mary was amazed to see and listen Gabrile. She was told to be a virgin, spiritual mother. She was selection of God. Mary deserved it. Mary was blossoming beauty at thirteen. An unusual light, unseen and unimagined, had entered Mary. She observed and felt it. It was happening with her. When she was taking bath at home. She was pregnant. She felt it. Mary was pleasant. She shared this experience with Elizabeth-wife of Zikria. Elizabeth was also pregnant. Zikria was at eighty. Mary and Elizabeth shared experience of pregnancy. Mary had been selected by God. It was opinion of Elizabeth for Mary. Mary was only woman on earth with concept of slavery and anti-slavery struggle. God had selected her for struggle of freedom. It was because of her anti-slavery concept. God had chosed her. She was in consultation with Elizabeth and Zikria. Mary was a woman with narrative of freedom. She was a saint with knowledge of social history. Slavery had reached climax. It was a culture developed by the Narrative of mythology. It was to be replaced with freedom. Mary was to develop the Narrative and movement of freedom. Angel Gabrile was sent by God. Gabrile met Mary to inform her that she was selected by God- for movement of freedom. It was age of slavery. A female could not lead any social movement. Female had lost freedom and status in the culture of slavery. Only male could walk and talk against slavery. Mary was given Jesus. Implantation of Jesus was implantation of freedom. Mary was genius. Mary knew- she had to prepare Jesus against slavery. Jesus was born for freedom of slaves. He was not a traditional birth. Mary was not a traditional mother Jesus was 4 years. Mary migrated to Egypt. Jesus was in danger at Galilee. Egypt of Cleopatra was safe home for Mary and family. She could preach narrative of freedom in Egypt. Elite of Egypt supported Mary and family. The elite supported narrative of freedom presented by Mary. Egyptian elite wanted movement against Romans. Mary lived in Egypt for 8 years. She educated Jesus in Egypt. She educated Jesus in history of slavery and right of freedom. She taught him narrative of freedom. Mary prepared Jesus for movement of freedom. Mary introduced narrative of freedom in Egypt and found favor. It was right time and space. Mary was right in choice of Egypt. Egypt had been conquered by Octavian. Egyptian elite had not forgotten suicide of Cleopatra. Wounds of the elite were still alive. Egyptian welcomed narrative of freedom. Mary negated Jupiter-Chief god of Romans. Egyptian elite appreciated and favored the Narrative of freedom. Mary developed and preached concept of monism. She negated narrative of Jupiter. Egypt developed into center of Monism movement. Moses-prophet of Jews had introduced narrative of monism in Egypt-almost thousand years before Christ. Jews in Jerusalem had compromised with Romans. Judaism was modified by religious scholars in Jerusalem. Jewish elite had compromised for economic benefits. They had adapted to rule of Romans. Egypt was different. Text and concept of Judaism remained pure and original in Egyptian institutions. Egypt was birth place of Moses. Moses preached narrative of monism in Egypt. The Egypt was right place to learn the teachings of Moses. Mary was aware of fact. She migrated to Egypt when Jesus was four years in age. It was right time of education. Jesus was taught in Egypt for eight years. Mary did it properly. Mary had educated Jesus for movement of monism. She was satisfied on education of Jesus. Egyptian elite had agreed with Mary on the narrative of freedom. It was Christianity. It was narrative to mobilize masses for freedom. Judaism had been limited as tribal religion. It stands same. Judaism could not be adopted by non-Jews. Mary reformed it. She developed Christianity. She made it a popular religion. It was meant for freedom of masses. Narrative of Christianity negated Jupiter and developed monism. Christianity negated worship of idols. It was negation of Roman mythology. Narrative of Christianity was developed by Mary in Egypt. It was narrative of freedom. It was religion of freedom. It was welcomed by slaves. Mary returned to home town in Galilee. Jesus was prepared to lead the movement of freedom against the empire of slavery. Jesus was to fight the war of freedom. He was to fight anti-slavery war. Jesus started teaching and preaching. Campaign was kept secret. Jesus travelled long distances. He conducted secret meetings with slaves. He organized people in freedom movement. It was hard. Jesus worked hard for years. Slaves were weak and afraid of Romans. Elite was beneficiary of system. Jesus worked secretly for years. He found a few followers. However, the message of freedom was introduced in the culture of slavery. Seed of freedom had been sowed by Jesus. It was to germinate and develop into plant. It was to mature. It was to bear fruit of freedom. Slaves wanted to eat the sweet fruit. They were unaware of the taste. They were afraid of the masters. Freedom was made for masters- slaves had been told. There was fear in slaves. Jesus had to fight against fear of masters. He decided to announce rebellion against mythology and slavery. It needed sacrifice of life. Jesus decided to sacrifice of life for freedom of slaves. He announced rebellion against Jupiter. Jesus began to hold public meetings at 23-years of age. He was young man of God. Jesus started teaching and preaching in open public meetings meetings. He travelled to towns and villages of Galilee.

He was holding meetings with the people to teach narrative of freedom. Jesus was negating slavery. He was negating Roman mythology. He was negating Jupiter. Jesus was openly negating the rule of Romans. He was negating the culture of master-slave relation. He was not to be spared. He knew. He was to kill the slavery. He was ready for punishment. It worked. Movement developed. It appeared as movement of freedom in Galilee. It was noticed by the Romans as a rebellion. It was different and difficult to control. Romans opposed Jesus on the basis of religious grounds. Jewish elite supported Romans. Jews elite objected on the popular narrative of religion-presented by Jesus. Romans were to save the Jupiter. Jews elite and Romans were opposing anti-slavery movement-in reality. Jesus was demolishing slavery. He was demolishing the empire of slavery. It developed into an issue of state. People were joining movement of freedom. Egyptian elite was standing with support. Contradictions developed strong. Roman empire was concerned. Christianity had developed into threat. Narrative of mythology was challenged. Seed o freedom had germinated. Christianity was spreading as popular religion. It was a great movement of history. It was to change culture and social system. It was to terminate slavery. Narrative of slavery was under attack. Romans used different ways to control the movement of Christianity. They failed. Romans decided to use state power. They declared Jesus rebel of religion. Jews elite supported state opinion against Jesus. Jesus was tried and punished. He was crucified. Jesus was crucified at 33-years of age. A large number of followers were there at mount olive. Mary was there to see the crucifixion. She knew what was happening. She knew what was to happen. Crucifixion could not stop the movement. Mary developed it into a system of Christianity. Church was developed. It was a centre for teaching and preaching of freedom. Religious organization was developed. It provided alternative system. Alternative social system and organization was developed. Alternative narrative was developed. Church was made centre of freedom. Women devoted for Christianity. Church network spread in Roman Empire. Mary died in 43 AD. She had developed Christianity into an organization on the basis of Monism. It developed into a popular force in the second century AD. The force of Christianity was realized by Roman elite. They had been defeated by Mary. Sacrifice of Jesus had worked. Soul of Mary was pleased. Constantine-the Roman emperor-adopted Christianity in 312 AD. Christianity was adopted as state religion in 325 AD. Mary had won freedom. Narrative of slavery was replaced by the narrative of freedom. It was classical freedom. It was turning point of history. We have to remember- Christianity was not imposed. It was adopted. Mary and Jesus won without any war.

Classical Narrative

Saint Mary Developed Narrative of Freedom was Modified to Classical Civilization

She was Mary-the mother of freedom. Jesus offered sacrifice for freedom of slaves. Crucifixion of Jesus was crucifixion of Jupiter-in reality. Mary developed the narrative of Christianity. The narrative was adopted by the ruling elite. Empire of slavery was demolished. However, slavery was not abolished. Roman elite adopted narrative of Christianity under pressure of church. Mary and Jesus were successful in the war against slavery. It changed history of the world. It was the greatest contribution of Mary. It was matchless in history. Christianity was with narrative of slave freedom. Idol worship was eliminated. It was achieved without any war. Christianity was adaptation. It was not imposition. The narrative was not imposed by war. It was a miracle-in history. Christianity was narrative of God. It was made successful by the vision of Mary and sacrifice of Jesus. Narrative of God was accepted by Idol worshiping elite. It changed history. God was God for all. Slaves were equal to elite in the narrative of God. All the humans were equal to God. Christianity gave a God to slaves.

All the humans were equal to God. Therefore, slave was not less than equal in the narrative of Christianity. It was the historical achievement. Slavery was abolished by the narrative of Christianity. It was not eliminated in practical social life. The elite maintained slavery as a tradition. Roman elite accepted Christianity to save and secure themselves. Constantine adopted Christianity in 312 AD. He was wise man of romans. Roman rulers adopted Christianity as state religion in 326 AD. They had realized the force of Christianity. They could not resist. Elite succeeded. They adopted Christianity. They changed their religion for rule. The narrative of Christianity was accepted. Freedom was not accepted by the Roman elite. The narrative was modified. Slavery was maintained. It was not religious slavery. It was economical and social slavery. Church was adopted by elite. There was king to rule over peasants and slaves. It was age of agriculture and handicrafts. A classical community developed. Professional classes appeared on permanent basis. Peasants were the largest professional class. They were producers in classical civilization. Classical civilization was developed by the negation of slavery in principle. However, the narrative of Christianity was modified. The civilization was based on perpetual professional classes. The society was monist in ideology. Peasants, iron smith, goldsmith, wood workers, stone workers, masons, slaves constituted permanent professional classes of classical society. King was apical flower of the classical social tree. Classical society consisted of professional classes. The profession and religion was determined before the birth of child. Son of the farmer was to be farmer. Similarly, son of the ironsmith was ironsmith by birth. There was no institution of education. Father was teacher of son. Profession was family profession. It was not changed . Pope was head of the religion. King was head of the state. It was a classical state. The classical social structure was presented as the divine determination. The civilization was monist in ideology. All was equal in the religious narrative. However, equality was not found in social system. People were equal in church. Church was house of God. People were equal in house of God. They were unequal on the land of God. The classical civilization was based on morality. Morality of religion was accepted. In social practice, morality was respected. Poor classes and slaves were satisfied with morality. They were advised to follow the rituals of the religion. Poor classes respected Jesus, Mary and saints. Church and priests were there to teach the narrative of religion. Christians had to bear poverty. It was told as divine determination. They were taught by priest. King was divine selection. The family had divine right to rule. The king and family were sacred and choice of God. The classical civilization developed as synthesis of slavery and freedom. It is the principle of social evolution. The deprived classes were satisfied by the divine morality of Christianity. They had been denied social equality. Poors were associated with Jesus and church. They expected from Jesus and God. Classical civilization was based on trade economy. It developed classical society. It was agricultural community. Second movement against slavery appeared in Arabia. Muhammad of Arabia launched this movement in 610 AD. Muhammad (last prophet) was born in 570 AD at Macca. Macca was a town of traders. House of God was there. The tribes of Arabia were holding with Roman mythology. They were worshipping idols. Movement of Jesus had abolished idol worship in Roman Empire. The Roman empire had changed into the empire of Christianity. Arabia, Iran and India were not affected. The regions were not part of Roman Empire. Muhammadans attacked and conquered Iran and northern India. The idol worshipping was replaced by monism. Northern India is Muslim Pakistan. Southern India is still holding with idol worship. India is only country-in world associated with Roman mythology. India was ruled by Muslims for centuries. Idol worship was not banned by the Muslim rulers. Mythology of India is known as Hinduism. The narrative was developed by Areans of Central Asia and local population. It was a synthesis of Areans and Indian mythology. It is still working in India. Muhammadan law was based on freedom and equality. Prophet Muhammad announced manifesto of freedom at Macca in 633 AD. Muslim elite of Arabia developed empire of Islam. Muslim rulers maintained slavery. However, the idol worshipping was abolished by Arab rulers. The freedom and equality was narrational only. Classical religions developed classical culture. King was divine guardian of people in classical state. There was classical society, classical technology, classical economy, classical literature, classical music, classical art, classical judiciary and classical rulers. Feudals and land lords had social authority in classical culture. King was presented as shadow of God. He was choice of God in popular view. Aristotle was recognized as philosopher of classical civilization. Classical culture was negated by renaissance in Europe. It was 15th century, when philosophical authority of Aristotle was questioned. Classical culture was defeated by modernism. Movement of modernism developed in Europe. It defeated the resistance of classical narrative. Islamic revivalist are fighting to revive the classical civilization, culture and kingdom. They are unaware of the fact-it is history now.

Classical Woman

Classical Woman was taken as Woman Servant of Husband

Classical narrative was based on divine morality. It accepted spiritual freedom-denied social freedom. The narrative was explained as divine social order. Jews, Christians and Muhammadans developed it in to classical social system. They announced social equality-developed social inequality. Poor was told to be made by God. It was fate. It was Criticised by saint. Muslim priest appeared as guardian of Islam. Saint was declared anti-Islam element. Priest dominated. He was supporting classical elite-traders and feudals. People are equal in mosque -house of God -they are not equal on the land of God. The principle is working in Muslim society. It is recognized as divine order. Saint objected and criticised. He explained practical equality in society. Saint interpreted true narrative of freedom. He was opposed by priest. Christian and Muslim elite modified anti slavery narrative of classical religions. Jesus and Muhammad were owned. Narrative of Christianity and Islam was disowned, with help of priest. Saints rejected and protested against the modifications in narrative presented by Jesus and Muhammad. Priest punished saint with support of state and elite. Saint was demanding complete freedom. Priest modified it into narration of moral freedom, only. Classical civilization developed and established culture of semi-slavery. it was same in Christian and Muslim society of post-slavery era. East and west developed semi-slavery culture in classical civilization. Classical woman was taken in protection and ownership by man. Man was guardian of classical family. Man was only danger to woman. Man was to protect. Classical society was male dominated. Woman was not owner of property. She was property-she was commodity. She was to produce children of the husband, for the husband- Husband was selected by fathers. She had to accept the husband-selected. She was to produce and feed children for husband. Classical woman was to serve-she was to be obedient wife. She was dependent. Woman was supposed weak in body strength. She was supposed less in intelligence-as compared to man. Woman was considered half person. Classical woman was social Subordinate. She was honor of man. Honor killing of woman is common crime in Pakistan. A girl romantic with a boy can be killed by father or brother. Boy and girl-both-may be killed on romantic relation. No sexual freedom. Love was considered sin and crime of woman in classical civilization. It is crime in classical narrative. Wife is not more than shoes of husband. It is common opinion about wife-in Pakistan. Husband can change wife like shoes. It means wife is like a commodity for husband. Man is to sow his seed in the uterus of wife. He is the owner of wife as owner of the farm and crop. It is told as the divine narrative in east. It is accepted and applied narrative. Woman in the east is educated to accept the classical narrative. She is educated and trained to be servant of male. She is to be servant in her family. She has to be servant in-laws, after marriage. Classical woman was social slave. She was called servant instead of slave. Man was allowed to marry four women in Islamic law. A Muslim could keep slave women as wives-in addition to four wives. The tradition of regular and slave wives was in practice, in Arabs. It is working still in Middle East. Arab rulers married wives. They collected slave wives-from the regions, they conquered. Arab imposed slavery after the name of freedom and equality. Arabs generals were always interested in wealth, gold and beautiful girls. They liked to marry girls of defeated royal families. Arabs conquered Sind of India in 712 AD. Sindh is a province of Pakistan now. Pakistan consists of regions associated with Sindh valley. It is the land on both sides of river Sind. Arabs conquered Sind and imposed Arabian classical narrative in the region. They collected slaves and slave wives-large in number. India was with mythology before Arabs. The wife was to die with husband. Second marriage was not allowed-in Indian mythology. Wife was burned alive on the natural death of husband. The ritual was called "Sati". Man was not allowed to keep many wives. He was to live with only wife. The marriage was arranged in classical tradition. Males decided the marriage. Four wives and sixteen slave wives were burned with Ranjeet sing-king of Punjab. It was Hindu tradition. Muslim society of Pakistan has developed a synthesis in Indian and Arab culture. People like freedom promised by Islam. They perform rituals. However, people in Pakistan dislike second marriage.

Classical Wife

Classical Wife was Social Slave of Husband

Classical wife was servant of husband and family of husband. She was a servant of parent family as a daughter. She was to marry according to the decision of parents. A boy could raise question on his marriage. Girl could not. She had to accept decision of father. She had no right to see who was going to be husband. She could not love. She had to protect her virginity for husband. She was obedient servant according to the classical narrative. Classical wife was to live with husband in hot and cold. She was not allowed to leave the house of in-laws. Husband had rights to beat his wife. "The wives are agricultural farms for husbands. It should be tilled and sowed by husband. Husband had to sow his seed in wife". It was stated in the divine narrative of the classical religion. A woman bill was passed in Pakistan. It was called woman bill. "Husband cannot beat his wife". Law makers in Pakistan voted in favor to stop wife beating. Religious political parties opposed the bill. They wanted to beat the wives. Council of Islamic ideology opposed the bill strongly. They appeared on Tv channels. They argued with reference to divine narrative. After weeks, a member of ideology council was caught romancing with an actress. He was enjoying her beauty. He was praising her curves. It also appeared on channels in Pakistan. He lost his seat in council. Religious politicians want to beat wives. They do not like to beat girlfriends. It was interpreted by a scholar on the same channels. However it is a contradiction in behavior and psycho-personality. Religious politicians and scholars stand with classical narrative. Woman was honor of husband. She was also honor of brothers and father. She was honor of family. She could be killed by husband. She could be killed by parents. It was honor killing. Honor killing is common crime in Pakistan. It has increased in frequency. Honor killing is classical tradition. It is always on love affair of a woman. Love was not right of women in classical narrative. There is a popular folk tale of love in Pakistan. It is a classical love story, known as tale of Mirza Sahiba. Mirza was a beautiful young man. He was son of a land-lord. There was another land lord in the region. His daughter Sahiba was a beautiful young girl. Mirza and Sahiba were school mates and class-fellows. They fell in love. Sahiba told her mother. She was in love with Mirza. She was locked in house. Sahiba sent a messenger to her boy-friend (Mirza). He gave a message to the messenger for Sahiba. Mirza harnessed his swift female horse on the same night. He reached at the back side of the house at mid night. Sahiba was waiting for Mirza. She crawled down the wall and sat behind

Mirza on the horse. Mirza moved to his village, through forest. Sahiba was asking him to move fast. Her brothers could follow them. She was nervous and afraid of her brothers. They could follow to kill them. She warned Mirza. Mirza was young and brave. He had trust on his horse and arrows. They travelled a distance from the village of Sahiba. They were out of risk. Mirza thought- they could take a rest. They sat under a tree. It was near to village of Mirza. They were caught in romance. Mirza placed his head on the thigh of Sahiba. Her delicate fingers were playing with curls of Mirza. Sun arose in the east. Mirza was fast asleep. Sahiba heard horse tops. Horses of her brothers had reached near. Mirza could target her brothers. It was critical time. Sahiba was at cross road. She decided in favor of brothers. Mirza could target her brothers. She was sure enough. Sahiba broke bow and arrows of Mirza. She fastened legs of Mirza horse. Mirza woke up and found himself helpless. Sahiba brothers killed Mirza at the spot. There are other folk tales of classical love in Pakistan. People are fond of classical tales, poetry and music. People love heroes of classical love. Peasants are classical in mind and behavior. Pakistan is a semi- modern society in status of social evolution. People are modern in use of technology. They are classical in mind and heart. It is a contradiction in mind and behavior. It stands as a major cause of crime against women. Classical wife is not in love with husband. She is sexual partner of husband. She always supports and stands with her parental family. She is sympathetic to brothers. She is tactical to husband. "Foot prints of classical wife always lead to the parent house". It is folk wisdom in classical intellect. Woman stands with parents in hot and cold by heart. It is observed in classical and tribal society. Woman is organic part of parent family. A woman belongs to husband as wife. She stands with parents in critical situations. A woman accepts husband and his family. She does not adopts them. She remains attached with parent family as an organic tissue. The behavior maybe explained on the basis of social evolution. There are biological factors, also with this behavior. A classical woman is always other as wife, in laws family. She is taken as an obedient servant. I know it very well. My mother was a classical wife. I lived in my village. It was a village of peasants. I studied women behavior- closely. Wife is other- in laws. Any member of the family can beat the bride. She may be treated as wife of brothers. Unmarried brothers of the husband may do sex with the bride. All are married, if one is married. She raises mixed breed. She has to work in house. She is taken as a laborer. A classical woman lives in the protection of male. She accepts this tradition of protection. She finds herself weak. This attitude had developed in classical civilization. She was dependent in society. She was attacked by soldiers in classical wars. She was made slave by soldiers of strong army. Power and right of decision was in hands of male. Women were taken as property of male. He had to protect her. Archetype of fear and otherness developed in woman, in classical civilization. Woman is treated as property and honor of male. It makes behavior of the wife in east. A classical wife is taken as other by the husband. She takes him as another. She is living with others. Therefore, she remains with more attachment for parents. She is loyal to parent family. She relies on parents

Classical Love

Classical Love was a Struggle of Freedom for Love and Marriage

It was romance and spiritual love in the classical civilization. Sex was secondary in nature of the classical love. Classical love was spiritual romance, more than sexual activity. It was more than physical rubbing of organs. Classical civilization had different narrative. Classical love was different than modern love. Yes concept changed with the change of narrative. Narrative of modernism negated classical civilization. It negated classical literature, music and arts. It negated classical love, also. Classical love was based on the concept of sacrifice. Lovers were to live and die for each other. They did not possess each other. They recognized each other. They owned each other. Classical lovers thought, they were made for each other. Love was religion for classical lovers. Each was "god" for other. There was no space between love and worship. It was not different. They were separated souls, on land, who found the chance to re-unite. Classical lovers were with the opinion. They were friendly souls, in heavens, before birth as humans. They had found each other.

They were not to be departed again. Classical love was lasting. The relation was not to break. However it was unaccepted by parents. It was a sin in the classical narrative.

Classical love was a rebellion against the narrative of classical civilization. Saints supported classical love and lovers. Priests opposed. It was declared sin by classical priests. Priest was against freedom of woman and freedom of love. Priest in Muslim society stands against freedom of women. Classical love was rebellion in reality. Woman fought for freedom of love. It was struggle of women freedom. Saints supported freedom and freedom of love. Saints presented an alternative narrative. It was narrative of freedom in totality. Priests opposed it strongly. Priests and saints were on opposites. Saints was standing with people. He negated religious, ethnic and social identity, classification and discrimination. He negated class identity. Saint presented the concept of all alive and all equal. Saint supported freedom of love. It was violation of classical narrative. Saint was ignorant. Piest said he was negating religion. Priest was opposing saint. He was standing with ruling class. People loved saint. They hated priest. Saint was love of peasants. He was respected in poor class. Saints wrote classical poetry. It was popular in peasants. There was folk music based on classical poetry. Classical poetry and literature is still appreciated in Pakistan. There are shrines of saints in Pakistan. Birthday of saint is celebrated each year. People gather at shrines –

large in number. They celebrate. There is folk dance, classical poetry and music. Celebration is known as "Mela" in local language. It means freedom to meet. Lovers wait for mela to see each other. People pay tribute to saint. They pay tribute to classical lovers. Classical lovers are taken as heroes by people. There are tales of classical love and lovers. These were written by saints in classical poetry. These tales are outstanding part in classical literature. Tales represent the narrative of classical civilization. Classical lovers always met with tragedy. They were not allowed to live with each other. They were not allowed to meet. They were not allowed to Mary. They were punished by parents Love was taken as an attack on the honor of parents. Lovers were put to death. Tales of classical love present story of classical tragedy. However there is a lesson. Woman rebelled- she resisted- she sacrificed for freedom of love.

East and West

Change of Modernism appeared in Europe it changed East

West changed to modern. It replaced classical Narrative of life with modernity. Change appeared in form of renaissance, in fifteenth century A.D. The struggle against classics succeeded with inventions. Engine was a big invention with a big role in social revolution. There was industrial revolution in the mid of nineteenth century, in Britain. Change spread to Europe. It changed the Europe. Industrial revolution contributed in development of new economy and social classes in society. Women participated in revolution and obtained share in economy and social liberty. Society was liberated from clutches of the classical feudalism. Modernism was called as movement of liberalism. Women put her struggle in the movement of liberalism. Europe developed in modern sciences, technology, and philosophy, political and social system. Liberals liberated Europe from classical Narrative and social system. They developed modern society and modern state with democracy and constitutional rights of citizens. They developed National state.

Most of the world, other than Europe, remained under rule

of the classical Narrative. East was in the clutches of tribalism and classical narrative. It is still unchanged. Social status of women is different in the east. She is social sub-ordinate in male dominated society. Women in east are suffering. She is chained in classical traditions. Women in east is living under classical authority of male. She has not found liberty and freedom. She is not with freedom of love and marriage.

West inoculated modernism in the classical east. Classical ruling elite resisted. A contradiction developed. Modern Europe used force to change the classical world. Classical elites and tribal chiefs could not afford change. They had to surrender political and economic authority. They resisted modernism. It could not be resisted. Europe used force. It included use of modern military force. Classical world was defeated by modern Europe. India was conquered by Britain. It was changed to British colony. European nations conquered classical world and developed colonial system. India was colony of Britain. East India Company conquered and ruled India almost hundred years. India was taken over directly under British parliament after the war of independence in 1857. It was war against the rule of east India Company. It was a war to restore classical narrative in India. Modernism was with advanced social Narrative and social status. It could not be defeated by classical India.

Indian population had supported Britains. Classical elite

were at war. Peasants wanted freedom from feudals. They supported Britain in India. Peasants of India joined British army to fight against classical elite of India. Rule of the Britain changed Ibdia. They introduced modern education. Britains developed a network of railways. They established modern irrigation system. A network of canals was developed. Britains established postal system. They created and provided jobs for the locals. Britains established modern administration. They developed modern institutions in India. They introduced rule of law and justice on the basis of modern narrative. India was not modernized. It changed to semi modern country under British rule. Classical elite of India was associated with Britain. British government educated classical elite of India. Elite learned modern politics, democracy and philosophy. A generation of elite was educated in Britain to develop India into a modern state. Rural India was was ignored. Peasants in India were not educated. Rural population remained associated with classical narrative and way of life. The classical elite changed to semi modern. India was divided into Bharat (India) and Pakistan in 1947. The division of India took place on the basis of nationalism. The British parliament recognized right of national independence. Britains accepted tow nation theory. They ignored the opposition of Indian congress. Pakistan appeared on the map of world as an independent nation in 1947. It was democratic decision of Britains. Britain decided political dispute of

India on the merits of nationalism. It was after the second world war. Ottoman Empire was divided into national Arab states as a result of first world war. The ottoman empire was a classical empire. It resisted nationalism, however it failed. Arab national state got freedom on the basis of modern narrative. India was also a classical state. Indian congress opposed nationalism. Opposition did not work. Britain took a decision. It was according to the narrative of modern nationalism. Britain respected two nation theory about India. Classical state of India was divided into the national states in 1947. Pakistan appeared as a constitutional state. There was inoculation of democracy. Women did not find liberty of modern narrative. Pakistan remained a semi modern country. The society is to live in a modern style of life. The economy and life style changed into modern. It is because of modern technology. However Pakistan is a semi-modern state with classical mindset. Democracy works in modern society. Pakistan is not a modern country. It is classical in mindset. Therefore democracy does not works. Corruption works very well. Pakistan is land of corruption and rapes. India is very same. Modern elite has appeared in Pakistan. It is corruption elite. The religious politicians are modern in politics. They are classical in corruption.

Narrative of Modernism

Narrative of Modernism was based on Modern Science and Technology it negated Classical Narrative

It was a long jump in social evolution. Modernism negated the divine narrative. Classical narrative was a great jump. It had negated the narrative of slavery. Classical narrative was developed by the Mary, mother of jesus. She was mother of freedom. Narrative of classical freedom negated slavery. It developed in middle east with birth of jesus. The birth of Jesus was birth of classical freedom. Mary was the mother. Classical civilization was based on the divine narrative of freedom. It was modified and reshaped by the class of elites. They had to accept the narrative of freedom. However it was modified. Society was divided into professional classes. Woman was secondary in social status. It worked for centuries a

After the death of Mary. A change appeared in the 15th century. It was the seed of modernism, cultivated in the soil of Europe. It is known as the renaissance. The movement appeared in the Western Europe. It was movement of rationalism. The seed germinated, it developed into narrative of the modernism. The divine narrative was replaced by rationalism. Classical narrative was negated. Classical elite resisted change. Change is always resisted. Classical elite resisted modernism. Priest opposed the change. Philosophers promoted it. Scientist supported. Women participated in the movement of the modernism. It was a step forward to the social freedom. The classical narrative was facing defeat. New discoveries and inventions were lethal weapons against classical social narrative. Earth was not center of universe. It was discovered by Copernicus. It was a lethal attack on the classical narrative. Earth was center of universe. It was faith. Priest was defender of the faith. It was to favor the classification of society, according to the classical narrative. Classical society was classified into perpetual classes, on the basis of professional determination. Priest was guardian of the classical narrative. He supported the rule of classical elite. King was divine choice. Therefore he could not be questioned. Rational elite developed rational- narrative on the other Hand. They developed humanism. There were big changes to the classical narrative, which appeared in renaissance. Priest could not face with logical argument. Classical elite was aggressive to defeat the movement of rationalism. Classical courts punished Copernicans. Quantitative change against the king and priest was in growth. Kings were depending on priest and army. It did not work. Galileo appeared with telescope. It supported the opinion of Copernicus.

Observations of telescope could not be refuted. However priest did not agree to accept that earth was a planet of sun. He could not accept earth as a planet. It was to accept the defeat of classical narrative. We must remember that Aristotle was a classical philosopher. He had stated the earth as center of the universe. This opinion was incorporated in classical narrative. The ideology was not religious. It was Aristotle in reality. Copernicus and Galileo were not attacking on Christianity. They were taking a review of Aristotlism. Priest had understood it. He defended Aristotlism. They punished philosophers who objected on the ideology of Aristotle. Aristotle was a philosopher- who had supported slavery. He was coach of Alexander the great. Alexander established empire of slavery. Classical intellect was standing with Aristotlism. Copernicus presented the theory of solar system. Galileo supported it, with telescope. It was a break through. The classical narrative had lost ground in Europe. However it was standing fast in political and social system.

Contradictions of the renaissance, with classical elite, developed into war. The Europe fell in war between liberals and conservatives. Liberals were standing with rationalism. They were negating classical narrative in economy, politics and social rights. Liberals were in struggle to liberate society from the clutches of classical elite. Conservatives were resisting. It was a natural resistance. The resistance of conservatives was social inertia in reality. Classical elite was fighting to protect their economic, social and political authority. Women were to get rid of the classical slavery. It was the social authority of male. The invention of engine was bad fortune for conservatives. Engine ensured the success of liberals. It played a revolutionary role in development of economy. Conservative lords were riding on horse. They were using man power in trade and production. Engine was a machine to work. It was fast in production and fine in quality of products. Engine developed industry. A new production system was in hands of the liberals. Conservatives could not complete engine. Change was escalated in Europe. Conservative could not survive with classical narrative. Eighteenth century was with civil wars in Europe. England, France and Germany were in civil war. Capitalist class had grown economic muscle. They were fighting for liberalism and democracy. Women participated in war against classical narrative. She wanted to get freedom. She fought for freedom. Women participated in the struggle for liberalism and democracy. Women suffered, however she was determined to get freedom from classical slavery. Women played moral and active role in the movement of modernism. We may remember contribution of women in the movement of liberalism. She supported new social contracts. Women worked in schools, hospitals and factories to support. The days of classics had gone-Ruosu said. Democratic social contract was need of time. It is known as new social contract in history. Narrative of the modernism developed National state, with constitutional rights of citizens.

Women and Industrialization

Women participated in development of Modernism

Invention of engine was a decisive development. It decided in favor of modernism. Classical narrative was defeated in principle. Social evolution moved forward. Engine appeared in 1712. Eighteenth century was for development of industry. Industrial economy began to grow fast. Industry created jobs. Women joined industry as workers. Industry developed new classes. It produced a capitalist class. Women joined working class. She worked hard on low wages. There was gender discrimination. Women was employed at wages, lower as compared with male. Women participated in development of industrial economy. There was growing demand of working hands in industry. Only male labor was not enough. Women worked to meet the shortage of labor. She worked more than males to develop industry. Women was interested in freedom of family. She was interested to great of the classical slavery. Women worked as laborer. She managed home. She produced children. She served children and husband. Women worked as less paid laborer. Women was working more than males. She was in struggle of freedom- in reality. She produced children to provide labor for development of industry. Women played a productive role in the development of modern economy. It is very much evident in the history of social evolution. In Europe, especially Britain, hold of classical narrative was broken by the modernism. Social contradictions appeared in renaissance. Contradictions developed into struggle of survival between industrial and feudal elite. It was a contradiction of narrative with social authority. Women favored industrial elite. Women supported rationalism, modernism and secularism. Families migrated to cities and towns. Labor colonies appeared on outskirts of cities. Cities swelled. New industrial towns developed. Industry flourished. Economic muscles of capitalist class were growing strong. Women chose to support industrialization against feudalism. Eighteenth century was going to change Europe. Social structure and economic relations were changing. Social structure was in transformation. Women was working for change. New class of capitalist challenged political authority of lords. Contradictions developed into war. It was war between kings and democrats. Capitalist class introduced democracy. They promised rule of law and constitutional rights of citizens. Democracy was introduced by Greeks in fourth century before Christ. Yes- we should remember Plato. He introduced democracy in history of social evolution. Seed of democracy did not germinate. Greeks developed slavery. They established empire of slavery. Alexander the great, Olympias and Aristotle were fighting for Greek empire. The seed of democracy germinated in Britain. It was 15th century of renaissance. It was the movement of social development which was supported by women on the rational basis. War of social change spread to Europe from Britain. Women played active role. Women contributed more than males. She suffered more. Europe was changed. There was technology and development. War of democracy could not succeed without participation of women. Women was with major role in development of modern state, economy and society. We should not forget Mary the mother of Jesus. She appeared with narrative of freedom.

Women in Modern Society

Women was denied Political and economical equality in Modern State

Modern society developed in Europe. Women struggled and sacrificed in the rational movement of modernism. Europe defeated classical slavery. Liberal and progressive Narrative won the war. Liberals walked over conservatives, with narrative of modernism. It was social evolution. The evolution appeared and developed in Britain. It spread to Europe. Europe developed into modern in state and social structure. Feudalism, classical technology, classical economy, classical literature, music, arts and poetry was replaced by modern creations. Classical politics was replaced by democracy. Industrial economy promised economic development. Women participated in development of modernity. She struggled in establishment of constitutional state. Modern state developed in Europe with struggle of women. Modern state was constitutional state based on rationalism. It was the concept adopted by Rusuo which materialized to National states, in Europe. National state made a new contract with citizens. It promised constitutional rights of citizens. Women got equal constitutional rights as a citizen of national state. National state was based on the Narrative of modernism. It developed by the negation of classical state. The classical state was not with constitutional rights of citizens. It was based on the divine narrative of rule and rights. National state was a new structure. It consisted of national institutions. National institutions developed as organs of the National state. Women was a citizen with equal status and rights in constitution of modern state.

National state was established on the basis of national economy. It was produced by capitalism. National state was ruled by national capitalist class. They established national institutions. Elected parliament was law making institution in the modern state. Women obtained the right of vote. She was accepted equal citizen in modernity. Women participated in development of modernity. She worked in industry as a worker to develop modern economy. Women worked as teacher to educate children. She worked in hospitals. Women worked in all walks of life for development of modern state and society. Europe was changed in respect of social evolution. They worked to develop science and technology. Women achieved. She found liberty and rights in Europe. Women in Europe found the right of education. She joined different modern professions. Women achieved economic self reliance. She obtained liberty and freedom of love. Modernism spread to America and some other regions. It changed classical narrative.

Women obtained share in modern business. Women achieved enough in revolution of modernism. However more than enough is still to be achieved. Women is living in social system created by males. Political and economic system is dominated by male. Modern society is under male behavior. Women are secondary in social and economic treatment. Women is raped. She is to face sexual harassment, by employers. She is assaulted and convinced for undesired sex. There are many problems with women in modern state and society.

Weeping Mothers

Women is facing torture and discrimination in the World

Woman is a weeping mother in Pakistan. Pakistan is a semi modern state. Modernism was introduced by English rule. Pakistan did not develop into a modern state, after independence in 1947. India remained as same. Pakistan adopted modern narrative as a state. It is modern in constitution. Pakistan is a corruption country in economical and political practice. It is hypocrite country in social behavior. Pakistan is a state for corruption elite. State institutions are rotten by corruption virus. People of Pakistan are slaves of corruption elite. Women is social slave under poverty, corruption and classical social narrative. Political and business elite is corruption elite. State institutions are contaminated. People have gone hypocrites in behavior. It is behavior of slaves, in reality. Women is suffering most in Pakistan. Majority of people is living in depression and uncertainty. Women is in struggle of survival. Corruption elite is enjoying the rule of corruption. At the day, women are saving children. It is the August, month of independence. A child in street is at risk. There are child-lifters active in cities. The network has expanded to villages. Children are lifted from streets, gardens and hospitals. Sometimes, snatched from hands of mothers. Children are lifted for children trade. There are children trade centers in Pakistan. Nobody is concerned. It was said by a judge of Supreme Court. He was hearing for missing child of a civil judge. Civil judge- father of the kidnapped son was weeping in the court. Supreme Court has taken suo-Moto action on missing children. Rulers are not interested to eliminate trade centers. Judges said. Police stands with minimum interest, in peoples opinion. Children are kidnapped for sale of body organs. International market of body organs has developed. Corruption elite of Pakistan is in trade of body organs. There are many in poor families, who sell one kidney. They live with single. Child lifting has escalated in august, the month of Independence. Mothers are weeping for children. Ruling elite is on picnic in Murree hills.

A wife maybe killed on birth of a baby girl. Birth of a girl is not liked by husband and family. Mothers weep on birth of baby girls. The woman is disliked and beaten by husband. Maybe killed. I know four beautiful girls of my village. They were shooted by brothers. It was honor killing. No one was interested. They were buried, quietly. Women education is not liked in rural Pakistan. Rape is common crime against women. Most of the cases are not registered. Parents are afraid of police. Policemen find an opportunity to rape women in custody. People avoid to register rape case. They like to avoid the second rape, by police. Mothers can only weep. They weep. I know girls, raped in my village. They are now grandmothers. They wept, when I shared with them, the event and consequences.

Women are working as sex slaves in Pakistan. I refer rural women. There is poverty and corruption. They cannot earn bread to eat. Girls leave family- migrate to big cities, work as sex slaves. Cities are different in behavior. Here I refer the poverty and corruption in Lahore. It is capital city. Ruling elite has settled out of city. They live in personal states, established in superbs. There are vip colonies out of city, for corruption elite. City is left for public. There Is public behavior. More than sixty percent of the population is crawling below poverty line. Women are to earn for family. Girls are sex workers. Sex workers come out of houses at evening. Majority of sex workers observe veil. They talk with eyes. Modern markets are with enough sex workers at night. They are behind veils. Many girls go to sex centres. Mothers are there for pick and drop service. Sometimes, father may drop daughter to the sex markets. The sex centres are not legal, therefore sex workers face problems. There is blackmailing and mistreatment. Police and commission agents benefit. It is different in cities and towns. There is no freedom of love and marriage. However parents facilitate commercial sex freedom. Sex workers have to earn for utility bills. They offord other family expenditures. Cities are with modern and semi-modern values. Commercial sex is adopted in big cities of Pakistan, as a modern value. Women have commercial value in city. However, they are suffering from classical values. People know Pakistan as a corruption country. They have adopted commercial and corruption values of semi- modernism. Women of poverty class is suffering life. Police demand a share in sexual earning. Police officials demand unpaid sex pleasure. Criminals are other threat. They are in links with local police officials and politicians. They demand unpaid sex and share in income. It is public life in capital cities. Politicians win elections with corruption weapons. Local criminals, police and capital are corruption weapon to win elections in Pakistan. Pakistan is under rule of corruption elite.

Working women faces sexual assault and harassment. Women in Pakistan is treated with commercial and exchange value. She is commodity with exchange value in rural and tribal tradition. A girl with love is called Kari in tribal law. Kari means a girl in love with boyfriend. It is sin. Kari maybe killed. Parents of boy are bound to present a virgin girl to the brothers and other in exchange. If lovers find a chance to run away. The decision is taking by tribal elite. A virgin girl, from the family of boy, is provided for marriage in exchange. This tradition of exchange is called vinni, in Pakistan.

The virgin girls are used as a commodity to save the murderer. It is a tradition in rural and tribal Pakistan. Sisters of the murderer are married to the relative of assassinated male. The sisters are sacrificed to save lives of the brothers. These wives are treated as sex slaves. These are the events to make the mothers weep. Mother cannot do anything other. She may weep only. These are major causes. There are many other causes to weep. Mothers weep in Pakistan. Pakistan has developed into a country with weeping mothers. However, media presents a beautiful face of woman in Pakistan. It is the fake face.

Narrative of Post Modernism

Post Modernism is based on NANO Science and technology its negating Narrative of Modernism

We have to change the model of economy and politics. Present Barack Obama said in his speech. He was addressing the session of UNO,20th september 2016. World is at war. It is the Global civil war. President Barack Obama said "change is required". He was telling to leaders of the world. Barack Obama has completed second term, as president of America. He has ruled eight years. He has fought eight years, for change. America stands with major role to lead the straggle for change. It is the war to change political, economical and social structure of world. Donkeys have large ears. Donkey is taken as the fool animal, in Asia. Barack is with large ears. You may notice.He has ears more than normal. Mr. Obama is not a fool. He is a bit fool. It may be explained on the basis of biological characteristics. President Obama has led war against terrorism for eight yeas. The war was declared by George w. Bush, in 2001,with military attack on Afghanista. It was reaction of terrorist attack on America,9/11 fame. It would take fifty years to create a peaceful world, Mr. Bush announced in his speech. America attacked Afghanistan with coalition forces.War expanded to Middle East. It is now in eighty countries, almost including Europe and America. Pakistan, Afghanistan, Iraq, Lybia Yeman and Syria is hot zone of the civil war. It is war against terrorism. American state department and intelligentia established opinion, through media. It was presented as attack on modern civilization. Talibans of Afhganistan were told savage people, enemy of the modern civilization. Same slogan was adopted by the Neo-lithic farmers to impose the war of slavery. War is in process. It is Global civil war. Imposing of the post modern Narrative is basic objective of the war in process. It stands to establish the domination of Global capital, through Global corporations.

It is war of post-modern economical and political agenda, in reality. President Barack Obama has spoken key words. "We have to change economy and politics of the world. Mr. Obama told real story of the war, in two key words. We find that civil war, presented as war against terrorism, benefit Narrative of the post-modernism. Post-modernism stands to negate the narrative of modernism. Classical narrative was negated by modernism. Now the Narrative of modernism is under attack of negation. Narrative of post-modernism is negating modernism in civil war. Religious and secular millitahts are at war against the national state. National state is under attack. Narrative of post-modernism has been developed by the Global capitalism. It stands to negate the National state, developed on the basis of Nationalism. Militancy against the National state serves Global capitalism. Global capital is at war to negate national state, It is the only way to take over economy of Nations.

National state was developed on the basis of National capital. It was the constitutional state. National capital was the primary factor working behind modern state. Modern state appeared in Europe, by negating the national institutions It developed National, boundaries, capital, army, constitution, Parliament, judiciary, culture and national Anthm. National state appeared as a result of social evolution and revolution, based on the scientific and industrial developments. Modern state adopted Democracy as the political system. National state developed on the ideology of Nationalism. National state promised economical and social security to citizens. Barack Obama announced, in UN assembly, need of the new economical and political model for world. He supported the Narrative of post-modernism. It is the negation of national state and economy. Global civil war is in process to achieve the same objectives.

Women in Struggle

There is a third wave of feminism it is struggle of women for equality, Pace and Justices in the World

We are now in the age of information technology. It is post-modernism as defined in the history of social evolution. Women are found in struggle. They have to go in struggle, because of the crisis. It is the crisis of post-modern sciences and technologies. Yes science and technology is not basic cause of the crisis. It is system. Technology is always tool of development. System causes crisis. We the humans are once again in crisis. It is based on the Narrative of post-modernism. There is global civil war for negation of the Narrative of modernism. War is in process. Change is in process, which is leading to the post- structuralism. Woman is in crisis. Woman is in struggle. It is defined as third wave of feminist movement. Third wave of feminist appeared in 1990. It is when war of Global capitalism started, after the end of cold war. It is war of post-modernism which is based on post-modern technology. Post-structualism is Narrative of post-modernism. It is to negate the structure established by revolution of modernism. Nationalism was ideology of modernism to establish the national state. Post-modernism is to leave behind the nationalism and nation state. Therefore it is developing post-structuralism. National state and Nationalism is under attack. Civil war has erupted as a result. It is Global in nature. The civil war in press has many faces. The biggest one appears as terrorism. It the face of religious millitants. They are fighting for revival of the classical Narrative. They attacking National state. There is racism, ethnicity. There are religious, linguistic, cultural, sectarian and other contradictions to kill each other. People were living as peaceful nation. They are attacking each other due to breakage of Nationalism. It is wide spread. Africa, Asia, Europe and America. It is almost everywhere. We are eye witness of the largest civil war of history. Midle East is war field. There is massacre in Iraq, Syria Yemen. Pakistan, Afghanistan, India and Kashmir is in civil war. There was referendum for independence of Scotland. Racism is growing stronger in America. There is voice of religious and ethnic conflicts. It is post- structuralism.

Women are always affected most in social crisis such as war and feminism. Women are most affected in the war. It is because, woman is not is not in uniform. She is not active part of war. She is not with gun. Woman is attacked. Murdered and slaved in war. Woman is suffering war. She is in struggle her life and family. Women are migrating from the war zones to save their children. Many women organization are working to protect life of people in the war affected regiongs. NGOs and civil society is playing human role to help the ill fated people. This is reality with third feminist movement. We should support feminism to protect the future of life. Masculine social authority has to be terminated for safety of land and life. Social authority of male has been cause of war and crisis. History speaks with evidence about the facts. It states that social authority of male makes history of war and aggression.

Third feminist movement is helping women and families suffering due to war. Syria and Iraq is the most affected region. Families are migrating for survival. There are severe problems with immigrants. Women organizations are working hard help uprooted families. Third feminist movement is linked with second and first movement in social, economic and political aspects. These movements appeared in the age of modernism. History of social evolution states. Woman was in struggle of freedom long ago. It was Neo-lithic era with revolution in stone technology. There was major development in economy, on the basis of new stone tools. Neo-lithic was era of agriculture. Agriculture was adopted by women, almost 12000 years ago. It was effort of women to meet food shortage in culture of hunting economy. Women started cultivation of crops. It worked well as a supplementary source of food to feed the tribe.

A great tragedy appeared with development of agriculture. It changed the Narrative of peace into Narrative of war. Agriculture developed civilization of settlement. Farmers had settled in villages. The agriculture was taken over by males. Males developed ownership on farm and family. Social authority of women was terminated. She was changed into labor and labor producing gender of society. Farming development produced surplus grain which developed the mind for trade. Grain developed into a commodity of trade. Farmers and traders wanted more labor for production of surplus grain. They developed the Narrative of war to get slaves. They started war of slavery. Farmers developed a new social system based on slavery. Master slave relation appeared. It divided humans into superior and inferior humans.

Women resisted war of slavery. She fought with full strength against slavery. History of social evolution was at the turning point. Farmers dominated. They won the war. Women lost freedom. Women never accepted slavery. She resisted slavery and Narrative of slavery. Slavery developed into civilization. It developed in Egypt and Iraq. Greeks established empire of slavery. Aristotle and Plato supported and developed the Narrative of slavery. Romans appeared with powerful empire of slavery in history. Women continued struggle against slavery. Women supported and participated in war of freedom.

Mary was great. She changed history. Mary was choice of God. She was a genius women. She was a pious women. Mary was only women to defeat the empire of slavery. Jesus sacrificed for freedom of slaves. Mary fought for freedom. She won. She defeated slavery and Narrative of slavery. Mary was mother of freedom. Mary won a great war without bloodshed. It was a miracle. Jesus had sacrificed life to win the war of freedom without bloodshed. His sacrifice was accepted by God. Slavery was defeated without war. It was success of Mary. She developed Christianity as Narrative of freedom.

Social Authority of Women

Social authority of women may change this society

The aggression is only crime. It is male behavior.

I vote for Hillary Clinton. Hillary is a woman. It is the only reason. I support rule of women. Hillary may be a woman president for America. I am to vote for a woman always. I am feminist. We need rule of women. We need social authority of women. It is required to save the human species on land. We the humans are leading fast toward the danger of extinction. It may be environmental change. There may be a war to finish the human story. I refer Stephen Hawking a big mind. The threat of human extinction is growing strong. He says, we are at war. It is global civil war. The civil war has spread to 80 countries, almost. As reported, it is war for change. Pakistan is in war zone. Kashmir, Palestine, Middle East, Afghanistan are in war. Africa, Russia, Europe are tense due to contradictions. They face attacks by terrorist groups. The states are under attack. Unarmed population is suffering. Women and children are suffering most. It is a complicated war. The largest number of people are affected in history. It is a war new in technique. It is post modern war. Women and children are suffering more in war zones. Women are in struggle for survival. They are fighting for freedom in Middle East and Kashmir. It is the war for social change. There is global capital to change the world. It is fighting for global capitalism. Global capital is negating national capital. It is negating nationalism and nation state. It is war between global and national capital. The nation state was established by modernism. Post modernism is negating it. It is social evolution in process. National state is in process of disintegration. Women and children are suffering. Hillary is a mother too. She may think like a mother for other mothers. I support Hillary. It is support for a mother. Only a woman can think like a mother. Hillary stands for women rule in reality. I stand in favour of women rule. We need to change the narrative of life. We need political and social authority of women. It may provide us with peace and prosperity. Woman does not like death of children. She thinks as a mother. Male cannot. Women joined economy in modernism. They participated in business and services. Women entered politics in post modern era. It is after Second World War. Gene of post modernism expressed in social evolution. It appeared in competition with modernism. Narrative of post modernism dominated in Second World War. Modernism was defeated in West. It demolished the structure of colonialism - established by modernism. Post modernism developed neo-colonialism. Post modern narrative competed with socialism after

Second World War. Defeated it in cold war. We are living the age of social transition. West has changed. East is in process of change. The national state of East is resisting. However it is losing ground. Post modern narrative of freedom supports religious, cultural and ethnic freedom. It promotes struggle of freedom. The national state is resistant to protect nationalism. This is the contradiction between modernism and post modernism. The contradiction has developed into crisis of civil war. East is suffering. West is not problem free. Women in West have social freedom. They have to face problems created by male. Women found a space to play political role in post modern narrative. She found opportunities in politics. We may point out prominent women rulers. They reached the top position. Europe is the land of evolutionary movements. However some women succeeded to find the ruling chair. Pakistan and India have seen women leaders in top positions. They were not with any narrative of change. They served the narrative of modernism settled by the male mind. Benazir Bhutto in Pakistan, Indra Gandhi in India served the modern narrative of males. Rule of women appeared same in Europe. It did not change anything in social narrative. They served the social narrative established by male in the history of aggression and discrimination. Hillary Clinton is there in America to compete a male - Donald Trump. She is not expected to challenge the narrative of males. She is expected to promote the narrative of post modernism. Hillary is not with a different social narrative. She is not with the narrative to establish women authority in political and social system. I pray for success of Hillary even then. It is a change. It may inspire women to play active role in politics. It may lead to the women rule and social authority to change the World. Germany and Britain is under rule of woman. Hillary may win in America. Rule of women may lead us to peace and social freedom. Asia Andrabi is a woman in Kashmir. Asia is a daughter of Kashmir. She is the mother of Kashmir as well. She is active in struggle of freedom. I appreciate her. I pay tribute. I stand with women in struggle to defeat the narrative of aggression. Women have to fight against aggression. Aggression is the only crime in social history of humans. It is mother of crimes. Aggression is only sin. It is the only basic crime with us. We have to eliminate aggression. It may change the world altogether. Aggression is the only crime and sin which appeared in the past. We need law and punishment - against aggression. We have to teach and preach against aggression. If there is gene of aggression, it should be deleted from human genome. Aggression is male behavior. History of human evolution provides facts. Woman is kind and sympathetic. Biology supports it. Male is not a mother. He is with strong muscles. Male adopted aggression. Female is with soft muscles. She is with soft mind. Female is considerate. She is sharing and cooperative in character. Women behavior is made of reaction - in our society. There is reaction of male domination. Change in social authority may change behavior. Man is made for labor. Male has been using strong bones for social authority. It is aggression. Female is made to rule. Social authority of women may eliminate aggression.